Courageous Judicial Decisions in Alabama

DR. JACK KUSHNER

iUniverse, Inc.
Bloomington

Courageous Judicial Decisions in Alabama

iUniverse books may be ordered through booksellers or by contacting:

iUniverse
1663 Liberty Drive
Bloomington, IN 47403
www.iuniverse.com
1-800-Authors (1-800-288-4677)

ISBN: 978-1-4502-8347-2 (sc)
ISBN: 978-1-4502-8349-6 (ebook)
ISBN: 978-1-4502-8348-9 (hc)

Library of Congress Control Number: 2010919509

Printed in the United States of America

iUniverse rev. date: 2/18/2011

This book is dedicated to my parents, Louis Harry Kushner and Rose Feldman Kushner, who moved to Alabama in 1937 and made the choice to raise a family in Montgomery, Alabama.

Acknowledgment is made to Mr. Timothy Lewis at the Alabama Supreme Court Library in Montgomery, Alabama. His staff helped me immeasurably with some of the case references. In addition, I am grateful to Honorable Pamela Lee North 5th Judicial Circuit Court in Anne Arundel County Maryland for her many suggestions.

Other Books by the Author

Preparing to Tack: When Physicians Change Careers

Coping Successfully with Changing Tides and Winds: A Neurosurgeon's Compass

When Universities Are Destroyed: How Tulane University and the University of Alabama Rebuilt After Facing Disaster

Contents

Introduction

Growing up in Montgomery, Alabama, during the years of segregation with Jim Crow laws gives me a certain perspective that qualifies me to write this book. As a child growing up in Alabama in the 1940s, I became very attached to one of our domestic workers. Bertha, our maid, used to take care of us, feed us, bathe us, and supervise us as we played with our neighboring friends. One Friday after she finished her work and went home, she was killed by her husband, who threw a brick at her head. He wanted her paycheck so that he could go out drinking with his girlfriend. The husband came to our house later that evening crying and asking my parents to help him as he did not mean to kill her and he feared that the law would electrocute him at Kilby prison. My father referred him to a lawyer across the street. The lawyer was able to use his influence with the sheriff so that the murderer went free. The fact was that it was not considered a crime in Alabama at that time to kill a black person, to cheat a black person, or to assault a black person. Even at a young age I did not feel this was right as we all missed and loved Bertha.

A few days before my sixteenth birthday, December 1, my father and I went to see a movie, *Not as a Stranger,* starring Robert Mitchum and Frank Sinatra. They played the roles of aspiring medical students and young doctors and I was interested as I knew then that I wanted to become a doctor. When we left the Empire theater on Montgomery street, there was a Cleveland Avenue bus parked in front and there was a large crowd around the bus. We inquired as to what was happening and were told that a black woman would not give up her seat on the bus to a white person and move to the back of the bus. Rosa Parks was arrested and taken to jail. This incident precipitated the Montgomery boycott. A few days later, the boycott was scheduled to begin. Several years later after I graduated from Tulane University, I was attending the University of Alabama in Birmingham. While on the surgery service, I was called to the Emergency Room at Hillman Hospital as there had been a bombing at the 16th Street church and four black girls had been killed. When I arrived it was obvious that the girls were dead. For the remaining time that I was in medical school, Police Commissioner Eugene (Bull). Connor was fighting the black demonstrators with ferocious dogs and high powered water hoses. I feel I am qualified to relate the story of how several courageous judges were able to make decisions that in effect changed the southern environment and the southern attitude in Alabama. The book is about the transformation in Alabama and the South from the years of slavery to the years of the Jim Crow laws and the convict lease system to the struggle for civil rights. Initially, there is a discussion of the definition of courage and just what makes a judge courageous. From there the conversation moves toward a discussion of whether judges should be appointed or elected by the citizens. Then the book discusses judicial behavior and how judges think. Judge George Stone, Judge Thomas G. Jones, Judge Frank M. Johnson, and some of their cases are also discussed in detail, following the author's thorough review at the Alabama Supreme Court Library. Included in the book is discussion of the case of the Scottsboro boys, who Judge James E. Horton said from the beginning he thought were innocent. The experiences of these young men in particular played a significant role in the Heart of Dixie's transition to a new South in which all citizens enjoy the American dream of freedom and democracy. By reading the decisions of these four judges, one sees the history of the state of Alabama from the courtroom.

1
Coping with Jim Crow Laws and Customs

When African American citizens in the United States of America wanted to travel from one place to another prior to the passage of civil rights laws dealing with public accommodations, they frequently were denied the right to stay at selected hotels, eat at various restaurants, purchase gasoline at service stations, or shop at a few stores (McGee). In 1936, and afterward, a booklet was available that guided them to accommodations that did not insult them by denying service because they were black. By following this guide, African Americans could locate hotels, restaurants, shops, and gas stations that would serve them. By 1949, the booklet had grown to eighty pages. A postal employee named Victor H. Green conceived of this booklet, initially called the *Negro Motorist Green Book: An International Travel Guide* and later known simply as the *Green Book.* To most Americans, this book and the problems to which it related were invisible because they did not fully realize that if an African American family wanted to travel from Alabama to New York, they had to take their food and prepare to have difficulty finding a place to stay.

In addition to hotels, the guide mentioned "tourist homes," which were private residences made available to African Americans.

Calvin Alexander Ramsey, an Atlanta writer, wrote a play called *The Green Book*, elucidating this problem. Julian Bond, who now is a professor at American University said, "It was a guidebook that told you not where the best places were to eat, but where there was any place"(McGee).

Traveling on the roads of America could be exhilarating, but such was not the experience for many African Americans because they encountered "sunset laws" in many Southern towns. These laws mandated that African Americans be out of town by the end of the day. So in effect, getting out on the American highways was a privilege for white people. This idea was expressed in more detail by Cotton Seiller in the book *Republic of Drivers: A Cultural History of Automobility in America.* All of these guides and related books ceased publication once the Civil Rights Act passed in 1964.

2
What Is Courage? Who Is Courageous?

When one reads the history of the state of Alabama, "courageous judicial decisions" appears to be an oxymoron because there have not been many such decisions. Most that did occur were related in some fashion to the racial problems that have existed in Alabama from the very beginning of statehood. It is important that we understand just what we mean when we speak of courage. Sustained courage emanates from character, which in itself takes a lifetime to build. Courage can be defined as the moral strength that permits one to face fear and difficulty. Courage requires a certain amount of leadership, and this leadership behavior is admirable and excellent. Making judicial decisions that changed ways of living in Alabama during the days of segregation required courage. These decisions could have severe consequences for one's safety and could affect one's family. Yet despite the potential consequences, there were at least four judges in Alabama who made decisions based on what they thought was the right thing to do and would lead Alabama in the right direction. The judges whose names come immediately to the forefront are George Stone, Thomas G. Jones, James E. Horton Jr., and Frank M. Johnson. Before the four judges discussed in the book are introduced, consider the following extract from the book *Courage* by Gus Lee, in which Major H. Norman Schwarzkopf tells his troops a story:

"Imagine that you and the troops for which you are responsible are on an international border. The enemy can cross it and strike at you with impunity. But you can't cross the border. That order comes from the commander in chief.

"Every night, the enemy crosses the border to kill and wound your men, who are Vietnamese airborne volunteers in your care.

"Every night, you chase the enemy, but they escape at the border, where you stop, as you are ordered. Here's the question: when the enemy hits you again tonight, do you pursue them over the line? Or do you follow orders and halt at the border? Questions?" Hands went up.

"If we cross it, will it start a new war?" "No."

"If we cross the border, can we destroy the enemy?" "Yes."

"If we cross it and get caught, are we in big trouble?" "Absolutely. Your president will be very displeased. With you. Personally."

There were no more questions.

"Gentlemen, STOP or GO? Write."

It's pretty obvious, I thought. If I've learned one thing here, it's that you follow orders. Especially from the president. Right from wrong. Disobeying the president would be very wrong. OK. I wrote: STOP.

When the last pencil dropped, Major Schwarzkopf asked, "How many said STOP?" I raised my hand. So did most of the section.

"How many said Go?" The major smiled at the few hands.

"There are two kinds of people in the world: leaders and careerists. Leaders have character. They act for what is right. They would die for their men." His words sank into the chalkboards, and the wall.

"Careerists," he said, making the word sound like a crime against God, "are self centered, self absorbed. They act out of selfishness. They sacrifice their men for a promotion. They lie to pump up results.

"They save their skins instead of others'. Careerists can't really lead because their men do not trust them and will not willingly follow.

"The correct answer for a leader, is clear.

"You cross the border. You destroy the enemy to protect your men. You then take the personal consequences to your career, knowing that you violated an order but acted for what is right. You feel pride in getting court-martialed and being reduced to a private.

"Everyone's a leader or isn't. It's not rank. It's character."

"Major Schwarzkopf was not teaching abstract theory; only months before, he had faced that fact pattern on the Cambodian border. A careerist would have let his men keep dying."

"He had risked his career but had protected his people and therefore his priceless integrity and his authority to lead others."

And so it is with the various judges described in this book. Each one of them risked his career to do what he thought was right. In some cases, the judges risked their lives and the lives of their families by making decisions that they thought were the correct ones.

For a judge to initiate change in a society through his or her decisions, the judge has to be ready to assume responsibility for that change. A judge has to know when he or she makes such a decision that a certain amount of personal risk and sacrifice comes with making a difference (McGarvie 40–56). A judge has to be devoted to democracy and fairness for all citizens. The judge has to have a personal desire to improve the living conditions in his or her area or in the country. These courageous judges serve as thought catalysts for change and as effective change agents (McGarvie 51). "They are willing and able to take the risk required in change and to build the collaborative relationships that make performance sustainable." (McGarvie 51).

Demonstrations of courage are not limited to the battlefield, but occur in all phases of life. This book shows how judges demonstrated courage. A folksy definition of courage in life is seen in the following quotations:

> The one place where a man ought to get a square deal is in a courtroom, be he any color of the rainbow, but people have a way of carrying their resentments right into a jury box. As you grow older, you'll see white men cheat black men everyday of your life, but let me tell you something and don't you forget it—whenever a white man does that to a black man, no matter who he is, how rich he is, or how fine a family he comes from, that white man is trash.

> —spoken by Atticus in *To Kill a Mockingbird* (Harper Lee 295).

> I wanted you to see what real courage is, instead of getting the idea that courage is a man with a gun in his hand.

It's when you know you're licked before you begin but you begin anyway and you see it through no matter what. You rarely win, but sometimes you do.

—spoken by Atticus in To Kill a Mockingbird (Harper Lee 149).

As long as the world shall last there will be wrongs, and if no man objected and no man rebelled, those wrongs would last forever. Clarence Darrow as quoted in *American Dream, a Search for Justice (2003). by* (Sherman D. Manning, p 125).

Never do anything against a conscience even if the state demands it. Albert Einstein (As quoted by Virgil Henshaw in *Albert Einstein: Philosopher-Scientist*, (1949). edited by Paul A. Schipp).

Cowardice asks the question: is it safe? Expediency asks the question: is it politic? Vanity asks the question: is it popular? But conscience asks the question: is it right? And there comes a time when one must take a position that is neither safe, nor politic, nor popular, but one must take it simply because it is right.

—Martin Luther King Jr, *Remaining Awake Through a Great Revolution*,1968.

I swore never to be silent whenever human beings endure suffering and humiliation. We must always take sides. Neutrality helps the oppressor, never the victims. Silence encourages the tormentor, never the tormented. Elie Wiesel, in Nobel Acceptance Speech, 1968

3
Judicial Behavior

Prior to discussing the decisions made by the four judges, we should give consideration to some of the thoughts that Dorothy Rabinowitz, a member of the Wall Street Editorial Board, rendered in her book *No Crueler Tyrannies: Accusation, False Witness, and Other Terrors of Our Times.* She cites Charles-Louis de Secondat, Baron de Montesquieu, who wrote, "There is no crueler tyranny than that which is perpetrated under the shield of law and in the name of justice" (vi). She reveals how certain American citizens became targets of the American justice system, a system that they loved and supported. But they learned that they could have their lives destroyed and could be sent to prison for crimes they did not commit because of the hypocrisy and indifference of the justice system. In many cases there were people who defended them and demonstrated the courage to speak out.

As we discuss judicial decisions in more detail, a statement by Joseph C. Hutcheson Jr. in his article "The Judgment Intuitive: The Function of the 'Hunch'" is relevant: "In my youthful way, I recognized four kinds of judgments; first the cognitive, of and by reflection and logomancy; second, aleatory, of and by the dice; third, intuitive, of and by feeling or hunching; and fourth, asinine, of and by an ass; and in the same youthful, scornful way I regarded the last three as only variants of each other, the results of processes all alien to good judges."

According to Richard Posner, "The secrecy of judicial deliberations is an example of professional mystification. Professionals like it that way because it helps them maintain a privileged status. Judges have convinced many people—including themselves—that they use esoteric materials and techniques to build selflessly an edifice of doctrines unmarred by willfulness, politics, or ignorance" (3).

Posner continues, "The judicial mentality would be of little interest if judges did nothing more than apply clear rules of law created by legislators, administrative agencies, the framers of the constitutions, and other extra judicial sources (including commercial custom). to facts that judges and juries determined without bias or preconceptions" (5).

What are some of the influencing factors of judicial decisions? Although no list can be complete, these should be mentioned: internal constraints, external constraints, judicial philosophies, pragmatism, personality traits, temperament, personal background characteristics, and professional experience. In addition, there are strategic and institutional factors, judicial preconceptions, and the legislature character of the judge and commitment to legalism (Posner 12–15).

Posner says that there are several theories of judicial behavior and gives several references (19; for reviews of the literature, see Baum; Friedman). He lists the following theories: altitudinal, strategic, sociological, psychological, economic, organizational, pragmatic, phenomenal, and legalistic.

The altitudinal theory states that the judge's decision is primarily influenced by his or her political preference. But once judges are appointed, by and large most of them want to be a good judge and do not make decisions based on what decision would be wanted by the person who appointed them. As a matter of fact, some judges completely change their philosophy after serving as a judge for a number of years. History tells us that it might be impossible for someone to appoint a judge and depend on his or her thinking for a prolonged period of time. For instance, King Henry II appointed Archbishop Thomas Bechet as the Bishop at Canterbury, but because the king could not persuade Bechet, once appointed, to see the world in the same way with regard to religious issues, the king had him killed in December 1170. Fortunately, no judge in the United States today is afraid of that punishment, but this is an example of how, once appointed, a judge will not necessarily toe the political line.

The strategic theory of judicial behavior states that judges vote as they do because they are concerned about the reaction of other judges, legislators, and the public to their decisions. The sociological theory pertains to a panel of judges; if the members of such are of one political party or are of one sex or the other, these sociological influences can determine the outcome of their decision.

Not all judicial votes are determined by political leanings. Some judges are chosen when they are obviously conservative, and yet their decisions might become very liberal. History reveals that some judges who were very conservative made decisions against segregation and racism. One of the best examples of this would be Oliver Wendell Holmes, who was a known Republican but who made numerous decisions to uphold liberal policies and liberal social legislation.

Schauer writes, "Legalism, considered as a positive theory of judicial behavior, hypothesizes that judicial decisions are determined by the law, conceived of as a body of preexisting rules found stated in canonical legal materials, such as constitutional and statutory texts and previous decisions of the same or a higher court, or derivable from those materials by logical operations" (quoted in Posner 41). The legalist slogan is the "rule of law." As in Brian Z. Tamanaha, *Law as a Means to an End: Threat to the Rule of Law* 227–31 (2006).; "How an Instrumental View of Law Corrodes the Rule of Law" (56 DePaul Law Review 469 [2007]). quoted by Posner 41. So when people say that a judge's decision was within the rule of law, they most frequently mean that the determinants were things that it was lawful for the judge to take into account in making a decision.

When a judge follows a precedent of some court other than the judge's own, he or she is yielding to a superior force and is not making a political judgment. This appeal to legalism is most prevalent in the lower courts, not the higher courts.

Judicial behavior is in large part dependent on individual personality. Judges, like other people, see things differently and do not see the world in a monolithic fashion. Judge Benjamin Cardozo said, "We may try to see things as objectively as we please. None the less, we can never see them with any eyes except our own" (13). See also Wistrich, Guthrie, and Rachlinski (1251). Undoubtedly, the personal characteristics of judges do influence decisions, and these include race, sex, professional experiences, and political and nonpolitical factors.

Even though judges have a great deal of freedom and choice with regard to their decisions, most are concerned about their reputation among their peers. There are also some external constraints. For example, the judge has to be concerned about his or her reputation among those who elected or appointed him. If private judges or arbitrators favor one side or the other and develop a reputation for such, future clients who are involved in disputes will be reluctant to hire them. On the other hand, career judiciaries are present in most countries whose legal system is not based on the English jurisprudence system. These systems are staffed by lawyers who make a career out of being a judge, and these judiciaries are one of the nation's professional career tracks. Judicial performance can be monitored to some extent by checking the backlog, the reversal rate, judicial demeanor, and the complaints and compliments of litigants. A judge who is elected to a specific term and who must stand for reelection is subject to a performance review. Such a judge has to be sensitive to public opinion. In states that have capital punishment, the most egregious murderers are candidates for such punishment because an elected judge is more likely to decide against the defendant (Kritzer

423, 461–64). In many areas, the judge has to constantly raise money for his or her reelection and frequently that resource comes from lawyers. If as many lawyers pursuing medical malpractice cases as lawyers who defend medical malpractice cases contribute to the fundraising of a judge, then the elected judge is able to make decisions based on the evidence. But if one side dominates the financial subsidy for a judge, the judge may very well be influenced by this resource.

The selection and election of judges has been a controversial issue for many years. Although most countries do not have elected judges, the United States, Switzerland, and Japan do provide for some judges to be elected instead of appointed. Former US Supreme Court Justice Sandra Day O'Connor opened her September 9, 2010, address to the National Hispanic Bar Association annual meeting with remarks on this very topic: "No other nation in the world has popular election of judges, thank God, not everywhere in the United States does either" (O'Connor, Sandra—"Selection of Judges," National Hispanic Bar Association, Washington, September 9, 2010). On the other hand, Dan Pero of the *Washington Times* has written that George Soros, through his funded organization Open Society Institute (OSI)., has spent $45 million to promote the so-called-merit system of selecting judges, which will reduce the influence of citizens and their elected representatives when it comes to picking judges. This is a liberal progressive way of keeping conservative judges off the state courts. Thirty-nine US states recognize that 95 percent of disputes end up in state courts and that this gives judges a great deal of influence over our lives, property, and business affairs. Therefore, they employ judicial elections to require judges to assume office by the consent of the people (Pero, Dan,. *George Soros vs. judicial elections, The Washington Times, September 10, 2010)*.

The alternative to judicial elections is appointment of judges. Chief Justice of Minnesota Lafayette Emmet said, "If the people are incapable of selecting their judges, they are also incapable of selecting the man who is to appoint the judges" (*Minnesota Reports*, 97, 2). There are several questions to answer: Do elections make judges more accountable? Some say the answer is yes because judges thus are more in tune with public opinion and because elections are more transparent than appointments. Others say that elected judges erroneously prioritize public opinion over the law and bow to the tyranny of the majority. They argue that judges can be held accountable without elections and that they are appointed by democratically elected officials. Can voters and elections do a good job of electing judges? Many say that voters ensure that judges uphold the law and that elections elevate the debate. Others say that voters should go to the polls to elect presidents, senators, governors, and congressional representatives, but not judges. They argue that voters do not have enough information to make educated votes for judges. Furthermore, they think that an election delegitimizes the judge. Do elected judiciaries better uphold checks and balances? Thomas Jefferson had an opinion on this subject and said that "the germ of dissolution of our federal government is in the Constitution of the federal judiciary; an irresponsible body (for impeachment is scarcely a scarecrow)., working like gravity by night and by day, gaining a little today and a little tomorrow, and advancing its noiseless step like a thief over the field of jurisdiction, until all shall be usurped from the states, and the government of all be consolidated into one" (Letter to Charles Hammond, 1821). Unelected judiciaries are more prone to expand their powers. But others say that appointed judiciaries are more independent to check the other branches. Alexander Hamilton argued for the independence of judges (*Federalist* 78). He believed that judges should be isolated from the political process and that this separation would help them check the balances between the executive and legislative branches of government. He felt that if a judge needed help from a political party and needed its campaign funds, he might have difficulty making judgments against these same political leaders Do elections improve the quality of judges? One side of the argument is that the people decide about the quality issue. Others argue that elections are a distraction for sitting judges. Does the election of judges fit with the idea of meritocracy? Those who are pro-elections say that elections are competitive, open, and fair. Those who are against elections say that merit and not money (for election campaigning). should decide who is a judge. In addition, these people argue that voters in democratic elections have no obligation to decide based on merit and quote Winston Churchill, who said, "The best argument against democracy, is a five minute conversation with the average voter." (There is no record that Churchill actually made this statement.). Finally, which system commands the public trust in the judiciary? Although electing judges may seem to bestow legitimacy, some think such an election is akin to peddling influence.

4
Chief Justice George Stone of Alabama

Micajah Stone, the grandfather of George Washington Stone, settled in the part of Virginia that was on the eastern slopes of the Blue Ridge between the James and Staunton Rivers. Legend has it that the first white settlers who cleared and settled in this fertile area were "Bacon's men." These men escaped the wrath of Governor Berkley after the failure of Nathaniel Bacon's rebellion and were joined by others who fled the bonds of indenture or escaped from oppressive punishment of imprisonment for debt. Some were fugitive sailors who had deserted their ships in port and escaped from being returned to England in irons. Although the exact dates of their settlement are not known, the Stones were certainly in Virginia after the year 1740 and before the Revolutionary War. During that time, numerous settlers arrived in this area, so much so that Micajah Stone started looking around for other lands to cultivate. Another impetus for leaving was this area's proximity to Fort Cumberland and Fort Duquesne, where the British were in conflict with the French and Indians and from where George Washington retreated after a disastrous battle. These early settlers wanted a homestead, and they were not afraid of the hardships and perils of the pioneer life.

When Micajah died, he left his slaves and a great deal of land to his widow Apphia and his eleven children. The children continued to live there, where they married and had their own children. Young Micajah, who was the fourth son of Apphia, married Sarah Leftwich, who was the daughter of a family friend, and George Washington Stone was born to the couple on March 24, 1811. Rumors abounded that the lands to the south and west were fertile and available for settling. Lands in the state of Tennessee and in the Mississippi Territory had hardly been touched, and Eli Whitney had improved his cotton gin invention for separating the cotton fiber from the seed and the demand for cotton increased. Because some of the northern states had abolished slavery, the slaveholders in the North were selling their slaves to those slaveholders in the South who needed more slave labor for the cotton fields. Meanwhile, British ships were bringing additional slaves to the South, at least until Congress passed a law forbidding the importation of any more slaves to the United States. It was in this environment that Micajah Stone moved his family to Tennessee.

Going to Tennessee was no easy matter. First, Micajah Stone had to sell his home and adjacent land. What household articles he could not take or sell, he gave away to other members of his family and to neighbors. More importantly, he had to take those articles that would be necessary because there would not be an opportunity to purchase such things once in Tennessee. Besides a full set of carpenter tools, he took three planes, a brace, and several bits. He took a small blacksmith's forge with a hand bellows and as much iron as he could carry. He also included extra tires for the wheels of his wagons as well as extra shoes for the horses. He needed and carried plenty of nails, which he knew he would need to build a new home. Although he took only one plow stock, he included good axes, wedges, a scythe, a pitchfork, a shovel, and a spade. He also took extra leather and several jars of axle grease. Sally Stone took what furniture she could transport, dried peppers, peach stones, feather bedding and pillows, and all of her kitchen tools, pots, and pans. In the larger crocks she inserted seed corn, wheat, oats, barley, and vegetable seeds. In the smaller crocks she included flower seeds. Besides taking the Holy Bible, Micajah took his long, straight-bored "Dutch rifle" and had implicit faith in both items.

Micajah Stone went overland for most of the trip but perhaps went on a flatboat part of the way. He and his family were not alone because there were other travelers going their way, and they joined Micajah and his family as they left Virginia, crossed North Carolina and Kentucky, and entered Tennessee. They made their way on to Lincoln County, Tennessee, where Micajah bought 125 acres of land from Sam Watt in January 1818 for $1,200. With the help of neighbors, the Stone family built a home and a barn and started clearing land so that they could plant grain crops for food; Micajah figured that he could plant cotton for profit later. One of the highlights of the Stones' sojourn to Tennessee was the visit to that area by then-president James Monroe who had been traveling to other areas such as Charleston, South Carolina; the state of Georgia; Huntsville in the Alabama Territory; and Nashville.

While Monroe was in Huntsville, preparations were made for the Constitutional Convention for the proposed state of Alabama, which was admitted to the Union as the twenty-second state and as a "slave state" on December 14, 1819. In March 1826, Micajah purchased 100 additional acres of land for $250 in cash. On October 2, 1827, Micajah Stone passed away and left a will detailing just how he had provided for his wife and his eleven children. Each of the children were left with three hundred dollars, a horse, a saddle, a cow, and some furniture. George started thinking about his future.

George Stone had worked hard with his father on the farm in Tennessee. Soon George would ride a horse and go to school at a male academy in Fayetteville. When the Circuit Court was held in Fayetteville twice a year, George attended most of the sessions. He knew he wanted to be a lawyer and hoped that one day he would be a judge. He was able to find employment and support himself at a very early age and was in contact with a leading lawyer in Fayetteville, a Mr. James Fulton. Initially he worked odd jobs in Mr. Fulton's office, but as time went on, he studied law with Mr. Fulton as an apprentice and a law clerk. When he reached twenty-one years old, he came into his inheritance of $300, furniture, a calf, and a cow. This inheritance and the law profession achievement made it possible for him to seek the hand of Mary Gillespie in marriage.

While working with Mr. Fulton, George Stone was observant of the political atmosphere in the country. The people of Fayetteville complained about the "Missouri Compromise" that had been enacted in 1820, just a few months after Alabama was admitted to the Union. At that time there were twenty-two states: eleven free states and eleven slave states. The attempt to prevent slavery in Missouri was defeated, and Maine was admitted as a free state, which preserved the balance. The Missouri Compromise prohibited slavery in all the rest of the Louisiana Purchase north of 36°30', which meant that the larger portion of the area went to the North. Initially, in 1820, this did not seem serious, but by 1828 it was causing a great deal of dissatisfaction in the South. Then Congress passed the Tariff Act of 1828, which the South felt was very protective of the North and yet put a burden on the South for the benefit of the Northern states. Thus the South renamed this the "tariff of abominations."Sentiments and animosity toward the North were running high throughout the South. John C. Calhoun, a senator from South Carolina, published his "Exposition" in which he declared that the federal Constitution was a contract between sovereign states, and each state was to be the final judge of whether or not the federal Congress had invaded the rights of each of the sovereign states. Virginia and Kentucky passed nullification resolutions as well.

President Andrew Jackson, who claimed both North Carolina and Tennessee as his homes, responded to Senator Calhoun's "Exposition" by stating, "Our Federal Union: it must be preserved." Thus, President Jackson informed all who even thought about secession that he would employ all means to prevent the Union from splitting into two parts. The Southerners had a great deal of respect for President Jackson, and they knew he meant what he said. In January 1831, William L. Garrison demanded the immediate abolition of slavery in his *Liberator* in Boston. This encouraged Nat Turner, a slave in Virginia, to lead an insurrection in Southampton, Virginia. Despite the alarm among Southern slaveholders, they united behind President Jackson and reelected him for another term. South Carolina remained defiant and enacted a nullification ordinance against the Tariff Act of 1828. Daniel Webster and John C. Calhoun began a series of debates arguing the issues of slavery, abolition of slavery, and the relationship of the states to the federal government. Because of its loyalty to President Jackson, South Carolina repealed its nullification ordinance. Roger Taney, who was proslavery, succeeded John Marshall as Chief Justice of the United States. Having a proslavery judge as Chief Justice of the United States was thought to be helpful to the southern states.

George Stone was concerned about these issues and wanted to take Mary to Alabama, but initially she resisted moving. Finally, Mary agreed to become his wife and move with him to Alabama. The Creek Indian nation had been defeated at Horseshoe Bend in Alabama by Andrew Jackson in March 1814. Realizing that the end for their people had come, the Creek Indians ceded to the United States all of their lands east of the Mississippi River. So either late in 1833 or early in 1834, George Stone went initially without Mary to find a place to relocate in Alabama. He chose a route that was a little longer but that was well traveled and safer than other routes. Other travelers at the time included gamblers, schemers, thieves, and some fugitives from the law. Stone elected to settle in an area that was initially called "Big Spring—Village Spring and the Battle Ground" and later called Talladega, Alabama. There he found plenty of Indians, surveyors, soldiers, settlers, and traders, many of whom were armed. Later, George Stone moved to the southern part of Talladega County, which was called Cleaveland's Store and now is the city of Sylacauga, where he made money by teaching. Later he went to the circuit judge to apply for a license to practice law. The judge gave him a perfunctory examination to test his knowledge of law, and with a letter of recommendation from Mr. Fulton, George Stone became a licensed lawyer in the state of Alabama. Stone took an oath to support the Constitution of the United States and also said, "I, George Washington Stone, do solemnly swear that I will honestly demean myself in the practice as counsel or attorney; and will, in all respects, execute my office according to the best of my knowledge and abilities." Now that George Stone had a home and a license to practice law, he returned to Tennessee to marry Mary and to bring her to their new home in Alabama. Stone was twenty-three years old, and Alabama had been in the Union for fifteen years. Even though the Creek Nation had been terminated, the Indians had not yet vacated the area. As a result, there were still disputes between the Indians and the white settlers and between the white settlers themselves. In addition, there was still a smoldering controversy between President Andrew Jackson and Governor John Gayle of Alabama. The United States had signed several treaties with the Creek Indians, and one of the treaties stated that no white settlers would settle on Creek land until the US government had completed its survey of the lands and made allotments to the Indian chiefs. But residents of Pike County had no intention of leaving the recently settled lands, so the US marshal for the Southern District of Alabama called on the commandant of Fort Mitchell to send federal soldiers to remove these settlers. One of the deputies was bayoneted, and the settlers decided to take the law into their own hands. The settlers were warned that they better prepare for a war. Governor Gayle organized the ceded territory into counties before any of the surveying was accomplished and did not follow his good friend President Andrew Jackson in yielding any of the state sovereignty to the US government. Governor Gayle said that the land was within the state of Alabama, the Indians were in Alabama, and the settlers were in Alabama, and thus the governor of Alabama would decide when and how to settle this land.

But the president and the secretary of war, Lewis Cass, ignored the governor and sent federal soldiers into Alabama, where they were to evict Mr. Hardeman Owens. Mr. Owens who had settled on disputed territory was killed, and this alarmed most of the citizens of Alabama, especially in Russell County. The grand jury indicted the officer and soldiers who killed Mr. Owens, and Governor Gayle ordered the state militia to intervene. President Andrew Jackson ordered ten military companies to Fort Mitchell, and the Creek Indians hoped that somehow a fight between the US government and the state of Alabama would restore their lands to them. Mr. Francis Scott Key, the author of "The Star-Spangled Banner," was commissioned as an arbitrator of this dispute. A settlement was reached in which

Governor Gayle and the settlers won the dispute, and hence there was no further infighting. Mr. Key and Governor Gayle reached an agreement on December 16, 1833, the same day that George Stone and Mary were married.

George Stone's practice consisted of small criminal cases and land disputes. His professional life revolved around the courthouse at Talladega, Alabama. At that time, there were eleven other lawyers, and three of them became chief justices for the Supreme Court of the state of Alabama, namely W. P. Chilton, Samuel Rice, and George Stone. Mary and George attended church in Talladega, but Mary quit traveling anywhere in rural Alabama with George when she became pregnant. George tried not to travel alone because the conflict with the Indians was becoming more intense. The Indians had sold their lands and spent their money and now were marauding the white settlers. Travel to Wetumpka and Montgomery was very dangerous because of the Indian problem and because of the resentment between the Indians and the white settlers in Barbour, Russell, and Macon counties. The Alabama Assembly initially chose to ignore the situation, and the conflict with the Indians only grew worse. Finally, it became so bad that people could not travel from Montgomery to Columbus, Georgia, and many citizens of Montgomery were being robbed and killed by Indians seeking the recovery of their lands.

In 1836, Governor Clement Comer Clay of Alabama ordered Major General Shearer, commander of the state militia, and Major General Irwin, commander of the Fifth Division of the militia, to assemble. The federal government did not respond to Governor Clay's calls for help, so Governor Clay paid for the state militia with his own money. The governor summoned twelve of the principal chiefs to Montgomery, where they met in the ballroom of the Montgomery Hall. Chief Opoethleyoholo responded by using his offices and his tribe to calm the situation and thus saved the lives of many white settlers. Later the conflicts resurfaced, and then the federal government sent General Jessup to join 1,600 Creek Indians to fight some remaining hostile Indians. This was a familiar pattern employed by the American forces; i.e. using Indians against other Indians. After the Blind Uchee

King, an Indian chief, surrendered, the government troops captured Neamathla, who was the real leader of the revolt. Other hostiles fled toward Florida to join the Seminoles, but many Indians who were hostile Creek Indians were caught and killed on the border of Pike and Barbour counties at the Battle of the Pea River in 1837. This was the last battle between the Creek Indians and the white settlers in Alabama. George Stone was relieved that the Indians had been defeated. He was concerned about Mary and their newborn daughter being alone while he was off in the next town on legal business. Making a living was compounded by the Panic of 1837, which only made hard money more difficult to obtain. However, in 1837, the federal government reorganized and appropriated a large sum of money for the postal department, and fortunately, George Stone was named the postmaster at Sylacauga on May 27, 1837.

When Benjamin Fitzpatrick became governor of Alabama, he appointed George Stone as a circuit court judge on August 4, 1843. Within a year, it was necessary for George Stone to campaign for office. On the eleventh ballot, Stone was elected in his own right as a judge for the circuit court. Unfortunately, Mary died on September 12, 1848. George Stone served as a judge until 1849, when he resigned and moved to Hayneville in Lowndes County, Alabama, with his daughter Martha.

Not long after moving to Hayneville, George Stone met, courted, and married Emily Moore, whose family was very wealthy. Emily brought to the marriage a plantation, slaves, a carriage, and horses. Slavery, to George Stone, was authorized by the Constitution of the land. He felt that slaves were better off doing the simple labors of the farm than attempting to fend for themselves without any education or skills. But his thinking was an anachronism as far as the rest of the nation was concerned. President Zachary Taylor was antislavery. The abolitionists and Free-Staters were gaining in power. George Stone was worried about the country and felt that the US government had illegally used its military force to keep California from being a slave state. President Taylor was determined to keep other states free, including Texas, Utah, and New Mexico, and worried that the nation was on the verge of a civil war. As the atmosphere and the sentiments deteriorated, several of the states passed resolutions for and against slavery. Then in 1850, President Taylor died and was succeeded by President Millard Fillmore, who did not share Taylor's views. President Fillmore was friendly with Henry Clay and his compromise attempts. Sentiment in Alabama was very pro-Union because most people preferred to let the slavery issue simmer, accept their rights in the Constitution, and have peace. But they misjudged the intensity of their opposition.

In 1854, the Missouri Compromise was taken off the statute books. The Southerners thought that the natural course of emigration would then determine the political pattern of the new states. This, however, was not the thinking of the abolitionists, who were able to raise a great deal of money for their efforts to capture the state of Kansas. Henry Ward Beecher preached violence in the state of Kansas and spoke out for abolition of slavery from the pulpit whereever he could (Reynolds, Dave, *John Brown, Abolitionist, 358, 362, 382, 416).* The people sent to Kansas were well armed with Sharpe rifles. John Brown was also very active in trying to encourage violence in Kansas and encouraged fighting with slaveholders. Initially it seemed that the proslavery forces were triumphant in Kansas, but as time went on, more and more antislavery people moved into Kansas in order to respond to the proslavery militants. The first shots of the Civil War were thus fired in Kansas, not South Carolina.

In 1855, when Governor John Winston was inaugurated for his second term, the Alabama legislature passed a bill establishing public school education for the state of Alabama, but it also passed a law stating that it was unlawful to teach slaves to read and write. In that same year, George Stone was sworn in as the associate justice of the Supreme Court of Alabama. Emily Stone regarded their new home on the corner of Adams Street and Brassel's Alley in Montgomery, Alabama, as a temporary home, but George Stone had no plans to move back to Hayneville. After a brief time on the court, he decided on a very controversial case, which even today has relevance. The issue was whether lawyers should be held responsible for their negligence or lack of skill in handling a client's case. Obviously, many lawyers felt this to be a dangerous precedent because this might indicate that a lawyer should never lose a case. Stone ruled,

> It surely cannot be successfully maintained, that lawyers are a privileged case, not responsible for any, even the grossest want of skill. I hold that they like all other professional men and artisans, impliedly stipulate that they will bring to the service of their clients ordinary and reasonable skill and diligence; and if they violate this implied stipulation, they are accountable to their clients for all injury traceable to such want of skill and diligence. (quoted in Brantley, 108).

The reaction to this decision by Judge Stone was almost universal approval by members of the Alabama bar. Nevertheless, he conferred with other leaders of the bar and disclosed his reasoning in his opinion: "The connection of the other members of the Court with this case devolves on me the individual responsibility of this decision. The delicacy and importance of the questions presented, have prompted me to submit this opinion to several distinguished members of the profession; gentlemen who have had no connection with the controversy and no previous knowledge of its existence. They all concur in the correctness of the principles above expressed."

> Meanwhile, another court considered and prepared to give an important decision. The Supreme Court of the United States, after President Buchanan had been inaugurated, gave an opinion on the Dred Scott case. Chief Justice Roger B. Taney wrote the opinion that held that the Missouri Compromise law of 1820, which had already been repealed by the US Congress, was unconstitutional and void. In addition, the Supreme Court determined that the Constitution of the United States and its national laws protected the institution of slavery just as protected any other property. Congress could not declare a section or territory of the United States to be free of slavery, and by so doing, it unlawfully

exercised its power. Persons of African descent could not be citizens of the United States and were not entitled to bring suit. Because of the hatred toward the South manifested by the speeches and writings of educated people in the North, the citizens of the South realized that they were not to be protected by the Constitution of the United States in the near future particularly if anti-slavery proponents were elected. Governor John Anthony Winston of Alabama, whose term would soon end, with Governor-elect A. B. Moore taking over the reigns of Alabama government, knew what was coming and that Alabama really was not prepared from a military point of view. He said, "Long peace had rendered us indifferent to the cultivation of the military art which every free people should be solicitous to cherish and keep alive in the hearts of the young men of the republic." Winston continued by saying,

The Union is not with us of the South, a "paramount political good" however much we may and do desire its continuance under a strict adherence to Constitutional provisions and guarantees. When these can no longer be maintained—or when further aggression upon or denial or our rights is practiced by a dominant political power at the North—we have everything to gain and nothing to lose "by disrupting every tie" that binds us to the Confederacy (Brantley 112,113).

George Stone heard the speech of secession and loved the Union but was distressed to see what was happening. Judge Stone tried to avoid speaking out on this issue because he was a judge and tried to confine himself to his duties. He also had personal grief to navigate during this time, losing two of his sons to scarlet fever on March 21 and 23, 1858.

The people of Alabama, like most Americans, followed the Lincoln-Douglas debates in the free state of Illinois. Stephen A. Douglas was a Democrat and was held in high esteem in the South until he promulgated his Freeport Doctrine, which was a scheme to circumvent the Dred Scott decision. This break with the Southern Democrats would have consequences at the forthcoming National Convention.

The quiet before the storm was shaken by an attack by John Brown on the US arsenal at Harper's Ferry, Virginia. This attempt to seize weapons from the arsenal and arm the slaves, so that they could kill their masters and escape, angered the South. Many Southerners feared for the safety of their families and their property and began to prepare for war. They felt that William Garrison and John Brown were in partnership with other Northern militants to destroy the South.

The Alabama Legislature passed a resolution stating the following on February 24, 1860:

> Whereas, anti-slavery agitation persistently continued in the non-slaveholding States of this Union, for more than a third of a century, marked every stage of its progress by contempt for the obligations of law and the sanctity of compacts, evincing a deadly hostility to the rights and institutions of Southern people, and a settled purpose to effect their overthrow even by the subversion of the Constitution and at the hazard of violence and bloodshed and whereas, a sectional party calling itself Republican, committed alike by its own acts and antecedents, and the public avowals and secret machinations of its leaders to the execution of these atrocious designs, has acquired the ascendancy in nearly every Northern State, and hopes by success in the approaching Presidential election to seize the government itself; and whereas, to permit such seizure by those whose unmistakable aim is to prevent its whole machinery to the destruction of a portion of its members would be an act of suicidal folly and madness, almost without a parallel in

history; and whereas, the General Assembly of Alabama representing a people loyally devoted to the Union of the Constitution, but scorning the Union which fanaticism would erect upon its ruins deem it their solemn duty to provide in advance the means by which they may escape such peril and dishonor, and devise new securities for perpetuating the blessings of liberty to themselves, be it resolved ..." (Brantley, 121).

The Alabama Assembly adjourned after this resolution was adopted planning to call a convention in the event Lincoln was elected. In the meantime, the Alabama Assembly created several military institutions including one at the University of Alabama and endowed a medical college. In November 1860, the nation elected Abraham Lincoln as its president. He was the man who declared that "this Republic could not exist half slave, half free." As the nation approached civil war, and as Alabama proceeded down the road to secession, the justices of the Alabama Supreme Court did not express any opinions about the disaster that was ahead. After many meetings, conventions, and speeches, the question of secession was considered and submitted to a vote. The Ordinance of Secession and the Resolutions were adopted—sixty-one to thirty-nine—on January 11, 1861, in Montgomery, Alabama.

Afterward, the leaders realized that they needed a new state constitution. They labored on the state constitution and also worked on drafting a constitution for the Confederate States of America. Toward the end of the month, but before concluding their session, the governor and the General Assembly reviewed the Cadet Corps of the University of Alabama in front of the capitol. The cadets paraded before these leaders and gave them a demonstration of some of the techniques and drills they had learned at the newly created Department of the Military at the University of Alabama. The cadets were given a celebratory ball at one of the hotels in an atmosphere of excitement.

Although when the new Southern nation was born, George Stone was not one of the executive leaders, the leaders were his close friends. In fact, as the newly elected president of the Confederacy, Jefferson Davis, rode up Market Street to take his oath on the steps of the capitol in Montgomery, Alabama, George Stone was in the carriage behind him with Chief Justice of the Supreme Court of Alabama Judge A. J. Walker and Richard Walker. In fact, they all rode in Emily's carriage, and the driver was a slave given to Emily by her father. George Stone felt that Jefferson Davis was well qualified for the job and had the necessary vision. Still, Judge Stone was not excited about the future and was worried because Emily was ill.

In the meantime, the whole world was watching to see what the newly elected president of the United States, Abraham Lincoln, was going to do. Great Britain was watching very carefully because it was not beyond the realm of possibilities that these Confederate States would become part of the British Empire. When the order was given by President Abraham Lincoln and Secretary William H. Seward to fortify and provision Ft. Sumter in Charleston, South Carolina, a cabinet meeting of the Confederate States took place at the Exchange Hotel in Montgomery, from which an order was issued to fire on Ft. Sumter at 4:30 a.m. on April 12, 1861. It was from across the street from Court Square at the National Shirt Factory building that the wire by the Provisional Government of the Confederacy was sent to the troops in South Carolina to fire on Ft. Sumter. The war had commenced.

Several months later, in November 1861, the Alabama Assembly elected A. J. Walker and George Stone as justices of the Alabama Supreme Court for another six-year term. All did not go well for Judge George Stone during this time, however; his second wife, Emily, passed away on January 16, 1862. In addition, the Confederacy provided for Confederate District Courts but never organized a Supreme Court of the Confederacy. So it was that the final arbiters of disputes between the Southern states and the Confederacy had to be the supreme courts of the states that joined the Confederacy.

By the end of 1861, the Confederate army faced the probability of a depleted force. The Confederate Congress passed the first Conscription Act on April 16, 1862, and the second Conscription Act on September 22, 1862. The Confederate Supreme Court was established by the Judiciary Act of March 16, 1861, but the court was never organized. President Jefferson Davis signed a bill on July 31, 1861, in which he suspended the sitting of the Confederate Supreme Court. The soldiers who were already serving in the Confederate forces respected the Confederate laws and stayed where they were. But a large number of Southern men who did not wish to serve as soldiers in the Confederate army went to court to avoid conscription. The first such case reached the Alabama Supreme Court in January 1863. The issue was would the state of Alabama relinquish its sovereignty and permit the Confederate government to force Alabama citizens to serve in the Confederate army against their will? The facts of this particular case were that the enrolling officer in Montgomery, Alabama, Mr. L. H. Hill, had conscripted men named Willis, Johnson, and Reynolds, acting under the conscription law. The conscripts petitioned the probate judge for writs of habeas corpus to seek their discharge from the custody of the enrolling officer. The Confederate government had to have the right to enforce service in its armies, or else its days were numbered, and the government would have to surrender to the Union forces. Yet the citizens were asking the Alabama law to protect them from the action of the Confederate law. The Chamber of Judges gave an unqualified ruling in favor of the Confederate government, and Alabama yielded its sovereignty. Judge George Stone said, "I am of that school who believe that the Confederate government is one of limited and defined powers, and that great care should at all times be exercised, to prevent it from enlarging its powers by construction." Both North Carolina and Georgia opposed the Confederate conscription laws. Judge Stone said,

> Let us not weaken or destroy our Confederate power, by embarrassing that government in the manly exercise of those functions with which the States themselves have clothed it. This will neither destroy nor impair the sovereignty of

the several States. They are not despotisms. For certain general purposes, they have conferred on the Confederate Government certain attributes of their sovereignty. This no more destroys State sovereignty, than does the surrender of certain attributes of natural liberty destroy civil liberty. In upholding and maintaining each government in the exercise of its constitutional authority, each will necessarily be kept within the appointed orbit of its powers. This, I humbly conceive, would effectually prevent all collision of jurisdiction. It need not, and would not, interdict the comities and kind offices which belong to authority or exceeded his jurisdiction The.chief justice wrote a masterly dissent and stated that Stone's ruling was a judicial declaration that Alabama had the power to qualify the execution of the Confederate law. Because the Confederate government had the responsibility of conducting the war and raising the armies, he believed that the Confederate government should be the absolute judges of the means employed (Walker, cited in Brantley 159).

In June 1864, the Alabama Supreme Court decided the cases of W. C. Mays and W. L. Strawbridge. These men from Alabama did not want to serve in the Confederate army and claimed that they were exempt from military service in the Confederate army because they were "bonded agriculturists" under the Confederate Statutes (Brantley 163). The then-governor of Alabama Tom Watts did not think the Confederate government was doing enough to protect the citizens of Alabama, and on July 25, 1864, he ordered the militia to enroll and enlist Strawbridge and Mays, who still claimed to be "bonded agriculturists." The Alabama Supreme Court said that Strawbridge and Mays should leave their farms and join the State of Alabama Militia to protect the people of Alabama. The court said that the women, boys, and girls would necessarily take care of the farms. Justice George Stone dissented and said that the Confederate law was paramount and that the state of Alabama must yield to the Confederate government. This position was a declaration of policy for the Confederate states and against the state of Alabama, and this decision eventually cost Justice George Stone his position on the court. The people of Alabama wanted security, and they did not feel that the Confederate government was providing that security. The Alabama citizens wanted someone to fight the invaders and raiders and did not care about legal principles. Governor Watts led the Alabama legislature to overturn Justice Stone's position. It did not matter that Justice Stone turned out to be right because by the time it was realized, the South had surrendered the war. Justice Stone resigned his position because of pressure and the external circumstances. The new Alabama Assembly was planning to relieve him of his high office.

In 1865, the end of the Civil War was at hand. Selma, Alabama, was captured and burned on April 3, 1865, by Major General James Harrison Wilson. Montgomery was captured shortly thereafter but was not destroyed. Only some cotton bales were burned near the railroad station at the Alabama River. While this was happening, General John T. Croxton was burning the University of Alabama in Tuscaloosa. Shortly thereafter, General Robert E. Lee surrendered to General Ulysses S. Grant, and General Joseph E. Johnson surrendered to General William Tecumseh Sherman.

But Stone's story did not end with the Civil War. Approximately ten years later, on December 2, 1875, a new constitution was ratified for the state of Alabama. George Stone was once again called on to interpret and expound on the provisions of this constitution and was appointed back to the Alabama Supreme Court by Governor George S. Houston after the death of Stone's friend Thomas J. Judge.

The first case that Judge Stone heard dealt with the lottery (Sam Rice, perpetual opponent of Stone, defended Boyd). Mr. Boyd had been convicted of operating a lottery, and he felt his acts were legal. He claimed that he was protected by a charter granted by the Carpetbag Assembly on October 10, 1868. Judge Stone upheld that the lottery was illegal and that the Carpetbag authorized lottery law was unconstitutional. Judge Stone meant to destroy the lottery and to protect the people of Alabama from this evil prior to waiting for any legislative action on this issue. The people of Alabama were reminded that Judge Stone was the same judge who held lawyers responsible for negligence in handling a client's business and who upheld the central Confederate government in the conscript cases at a time when Governor Thomas Watts and other members of the court surrendered principles for expediency (*Boyd v. State,* 53 Ala. 601 and 615; Brantley 261).

Judge Stone wrote 1,931 opinions from 1876 until his death on March 11, 1894. In just one year he wrote 175 opinions. Upon his death, the Governor of Alabama said, "No man ever lived in Alabama who did her more honor; and none ever died within her borders whose loss was a greater calamity for the State" (Brantley 286).

5
Judge Thomas Goode Jones

Thomas Goode Jones was born on November 26, 1844, in Vineville, Georgia, a suburb of Macon, Georgia. His father, Samuel Goode Jones, was an engineer who at one time held a position with the Montgomery Railroad and the Muscogee Railroad in Georgia. At another time, Samuel Jones was president of the Savannah & Memphis Railroad and later chief engineer for the Savannah & Memphis Railroad. These railroads increased commerce for central and southern Alabama and helped the Confederacy transport troops and supplies during the Civil War, from 1861 to 1865. According to Walter Jones, Samuel Jones influenced Thomas Goode Jones in various ways:

> Mr. Samuel Goode Jones was deeply religious by birth and inclination and was a devoted and genuinely consistent member of the Episcopal Church, giving lavishly of his time and means towards its support. The first church service held by the Episcopalians of Atlanta was held in his home and was the beginning of the present St. Luke's Parish. The Rev. W. C. Whittaker, in his History of the Protestant Episcopal Church in Alabama, 1763–1891, referring to some of the splendid personalities among the laymen of the Church in Alabama, during the ministrations of Bishops Cobbs and

Wilmer, says: "Yet six men must be named, in passing , to ignore whom were to ignore six of the strongest pillars of the Diocese" and thus refers to Mr. Jones: "Samuel G. Jones, a foundation stone of Hammer Hall and of the original church of the Holy Comforter." He was ardent in his efforts to organize and support the University of the South, at Sewanee, Tennessee, and was one of the principal laymen who aided in establishing it (Walter Jones as quoted by Eidsmoe 19).

Mattie Pegues Wood lists Samuel Goode Jones as a trustee of Hammer Hall, a church-sponsored boarding school and room house for girls (Wood 46, 98). In Wood's book, she describes how when President and Mrs. Jefferson Davis arrived in Montgomery and attended St. John's Episcopal Church, Colonel Samuel Jones was the usher who showed them to their pew (Wood 53).

Samuel Goode Jones owned slaves, just as many Southerners did before the Civil War, and his grandson had the following to say about this subject:

> No man ever dealt more kindly with his slaves. He never sold one of his own and oftentimes, at the instance of husbands and wives , he would buy slaves to prevent a separation. His slaves worshipped him and seemed never more content than when performing service for him. On one occasion a slave (Sarah Ann). whom he had carried North with him as a nurse, ran away and Mr. Jones had to return home without her. Afterwards he received a pitiful appeal from her for aid in getting back to him and his family. And Mr. Jones sent her money to return. (Walter Jones quoted in Eidsmore 24).

In 1860, Thomas Goode Jones entered the Virginia Military Institute (VMI). in Lexington, Virginia. The records of his courses are incomplete during the war years of 1861–1865 because the students and faculty were away for the duration of the war, and the institution was burned down by the federal troops in June 1864 (McMurry 52,

70). The cadets were expected to help with the efforts of the Southern states during the war. Jones served in Richmond as a drillmaster of recruits in Virginia and was under then Major Thomas J. "Stonewall" Jackson, who was a professor at VMI. In contrast to West Point, the students at VMI were mainly from the South. The VMI Board of Visitors declared on December 12, 1861, that members of the class of 1862 were "war graduates." Although Thomas Jones left VMI, his father tried to make arrangements for him to return and on June 28, 1861, Samuel Goode Jones wrote a letter to Superintendent Smith. Thomas did return for a few months, but on April 23, 1862, he changed his mind. Thomas wrote to the Superintendent of VMI, "The State of Alabama has the first right to my services, and should the Corps of Cadets (VMI). be called into service, I would prefer to enter it with men from my State and County" (quoted in Eidsmore 43). According to Dr. Malcolm Cook McMillan, research professor of history at Auburn University, Jones "participated in all the campaigns of the Army of Northern Virginia after Fredericksburg. Six times wounded in battle, he was cited for conspicuous bravery at the battles of Cedar Creek and Bristoe's Station and, although only eighteen years old, was promoted to major" (McMillan as quoted by Eidsmoe 51).

By 1864, it was clear to most of those involved in the war effort that the Union was going to win. The North had more of everything except perhaps fighting spirit. At the age of twenty, Jones was promoted to the rank of lieutenant colonel. But on April 9, 1865, Major Jones rode out from the Southern lines with a white flag of truce and surrendered to Gen. Ulysses Grant (DuBose 9).

Sergeant-Major William Shore of Pittsburgh, Pennsylvania, was the first Union soldier to meet the officer carrying the flag of truce. Years later in 1902, when Thomas Goode Jones was appointed to a federal judgeship, Shore wrote Jones to see if in fact he was that officer. On April 14, 1902, Jones replied, and part of that letter is reproduced here:

When the war ended at Appomattox, I was an officer on the staff of Major-General John B. Gordon, who then commanded the Second Corps of the army of Northern Virginia and parts of Anderson's corps. General Gordon was selected to command the troops which attempted to cut out about daybreak on April 9th, and I was with him in that charge.

As the emergency was very pressing and your people were about to swoop down upon us, it was all important to stop hostilities at once, and General Gordon directed flags to be carried to several points along the line which was advancing on us. I was not quite twenty-one years old, and was mounted on a good looking bay horse, and was in full dress, having put on our best uniforms for fear they would be captured with our wagons. We all expected the worst and wished to be dressed as decently as possible. I rode in on the right of the Appomattox Court House, coming from the direction of our lines. Some of your skirmishers opened fire on me at first, but they stopped as soon as they perceived my flag of truce, which was a large, white napkin in which some ladies had wrapped a snack for me the day before, the napkin being all that remained in my haversack. I have always had a vague recollection that the officer I met was an artilleryman, and it may be you were the man who told me where to go.

It would give me great pleasure to meet you should chance ever bring you to Alabama, and I will hunt you up if I ever come to Pittsburgh (VMI Archives).

After the Civil War, Thomas Goode Jones returned to Alabama and to farming. Through his mother, he received a portion of his grandfather's estate, which he used to purchase a 750-acre plantation in Montgomery County between Sellers and Davenport. On December 20, 1866, he married Georgena Caroline Bird, who was a native of Montgomery. As the years went by, they had thirteen children. In the evenings when he was not working the farm, Jones read and studied the law. There was no law school in the state of Alabama, and the way into the profession of law at that time was through independent reading and studying and later apprenticeship to an established lawyer or judge. Initially, Jones worked with John A. Elmore and later enrolled in a night law class taught by A. J. Walker, the chief justice of the Alabama Supreme Court (Eidsmore 111). Chief Justice Walker believed that a judge should apply the law fairly and give deference to the "ancient common law" and the intent of the state legislature ("Tribute").

Although there is no record of exactly which books Thomas Goode Jones read, the University of Alabama Law School opened in 1872, and the following texts were used there: Walker, *Introduction to American Law*; Stephen, *Principles of Pleading*; Kent, *Commentaries on American Law*; Greenleaf, *The Law of Evidence*; Blackstone, *Commentaries on the Laws of England*; Adams, *The Doctrine of Equity*; Parsons, *The Law of Contracts*; Roscoe, *The Law of Evidence in Criminal Cases,* Roscoe; and the Revised Code of Alabama (McKensie 121).

Thomas Goode Jones was admitted to practice in the courts of Alabama in December 1866; in the Supreme Court of Alabama on January 9, 1868; in the US District Court on May 25, 1868; and in the US Supreme Court in 1876 (Eidsmore 122). Thomas Jones and his family lived in several homes in Montgomery, on Bainbridge Street, Alabama Street, South Hull Street, and finally 323 Adams Street. Some of his clients included Louisville & Nashville Railroad Company, South & North Railroad Company, Mobile & Montgomery Railroad Company, Standard Oil, Western Union Telegraph Company, the Southern Express Company, and Capital City Water Works Company (Eidsmore 123).

Jones also served as editor of the *Daily Picayune,* a small Montgomery newspaper, from June through November

1868. In order to really understand this man, it is helpful to read some of his editorials, including the following:

Our mission is simple and noble. The ravages of war and the miseries of a doubtful peace, have well nigh ruined our once prosperous "Sunny South." As living sons, who cling with fond affections to the land of our birth, we will endeavor,—as far as in us lies—to do our full share in bringing back former prosperity and happiness. The bone and sinew of a country is to labor. To build up a torn and shattered state, we must foster and cherish every principle which tends to elevate and strengthen its working men. The divine mandate to our first ancestor, that his "bread should be eaten only by the sweat of his brow," is one that cannot be safely disregarded, even now. History tells, with startling emphasis, the fate of nations, which favored by fortune have gained prosperity and wealth, without toil and labor. Vice and degeneracy have followed fast upon the foot-steps of wealth, to give wing in turn to factions, bloodshed, famine and misrule—then wealth without a solid basis "takes unto itself wings and flies away," often, descendents of wealthy ancestors, from the stern strength imparted to manhood by trial, build up honor and greatness amidst the ruins and ashes and woe follow such prosperity—and we may safely say that *for every generation which has enjoyed prosperity and wealth without labor, two generations have atoned for it in poverty and misery* (Jones, *Salutation*, Daily Picayune, 2, June 11, 1868, as quoted in Eidsmoe 128–129).

On June 24, 1868, he wrote,

The issues upon which we fought are dead, slavery and secession are buried with the past; but the *"idea,"* the *"principles,"* that freedmen have a right to govern themselves and to resist tyrants, will never die on this continent, as long as Anglo-Saxon blood runs in our veins. The memory of our slain countrymen will *never* lie buried ("Northern Immigration," *Daily Picayune* as quoted by Eidsmoe 135).

Thomas Goode Jones felt that the idea of a Ku Klux Klan was a silly one and not to be taken seriously:

As to the Ku Klux Klan—it was the concoction, we think, of a few thoughtless young men, who from a desire for fun, worked on the superstition of one class of our citizens. The press of the South gave currency to the idea, and the political opponents of the South took advantage of the circumstance to charge every crime in the community, upon the Ku Klux Klan. The writer of this article would have had abundant opportunity to know if such an organization ever existed in Montgomery. We have never yet seen or heard of any one who was Ku Klux Klan (*Daily Picayune,* July 9, 1868).

Perhaps the most significant contribution to the legal profession made by Thomas Goode Jones was the first code of ethics that he wrote, which was the first code of ethics adopted by any bar in America. He was very much influenced by George Sharswood, who in 1854 had written "An Essay on Professional Ethics." Jones began his code with a quotation from Sharswood's essay: "There is, perhaps, no profession after that of the sacred ministry, in which a high-toned morality is more imperatively necessary than that of the law. There is certainly, without any exception, no profession in which so many temptations beset the path to swerve from the lines of strict integrity; in which so many delicate and difficult questions of duty are constantly arising. There are pitfalls and man-traps at every step, and the mere youth, at the very outset of his career, needs often the prudence and self-denial, as well as the moral courage, which belongs commonly to riper years. High moral principle is his only safe guide; the only torch to light his way amidst darkness and obstruction" (Sharswood as quoted in Code of Ethics, Alabama State Bar Association 1887, reprinted from 2 Ala. Law 3 July 1941, at 259, quoted by Eidsmoe 157).

At this time, the American Bar Association moved forward to draft its own code of ethics for the nation. But when its leaders read what Jones had written for Alabama, which had been adopted already by ten other states, they used most of the Alabama Code of Ethics. Colonel Thomas Hamlin Hubbard of New York City, who presented the report to the Committee on a Code of Professional Ethics, stated, "The report which I now present gives the Alabama Code and the variations made by the ten associations other than the association of the State of Alabama that have followed it. So that you have before you in this report, as we think, the substance of all that is needed to prepare canons of ethics and you have in the main a form which may safely be adopted; for manifestly, it is safer to follow a good precedent if one has been made than to establish a new one" (Horton 130).

The Reconstruction Era ended in 1875 when the Union troops departed and the South was allowed to govern its own affairs. But the South still continued to be isolated from the rest of the nation until 1940. One person who served as a bridge between the North and the South during this time was Thomas Goode Jones.

Thomas Jones held liberal attitudes on racial issues and opposed bills that would have subjected black farmers to peonage or imprisonment for debt. He opposed the fee system by which sheriffs and other law enforcement officers were paid depending on the number of black convicts they leased out. But the convict lease system added to the revenues of the state of Alabama and the politicians were reluctant to relinquish that income for the state. In 1886, Thomas Jones was speaker of the House of Representatives of the Alabama legislature. While serving in this capacity, he was opposed to ties with labor groups, but he supported child labor laws. He was very much opposed to lynching but was not able to have much influence with the 1875 constitutional convention. Jones pushed for laws to impeach any sheriff who allowed his prisoners to be seized by a lynch mob.

The issue of lynching was a very important one to Judge Thomas Jones because of its disregard for lawful authority and the legal process. He wrestled with the question of whether there was constitutional authority for a federal statute that made lynching in a county jail a federal crime. In one case, Horace Maples had been arrested and incarcerated in the Madison County jail when, on September 7, 1904, a mob of white persons snatched Maples from the jail and lynched him. Thomas Riggins, who was part of this mob, was arrested and charged with violating sections 5508 and 5509 of the Revised Statutes of the United States, which stated that it was a crime to violate the civil rights of a citizen of the United States. Riggins filed a petition for a writ of habeas corpus on the ground that sections 5508 and 5509 were not authorized by the US Constitution.

In his ruling in the case, Judge Jones said, "The Fourteenth Amendment Section I says that no State can deprive any person of life, liberty, or property, without due process of law; nor deny to any person within its jurisdiction the equal protection of the laws" (US Const. Amend. XIV 1). Jones wrote also, "The phrase due process has had a well defined meaning for ages. It has been previously employed in the Fifth Amendment. Putting it in the Fourteenth Amendment not only granted, but directly defined, certain specific rights which inure to the benefit of every person, alien as well as citizen, and are derived from, dependent upon or secured by the Constitution of the United States."

What Judge Jones meant is that Maples had the right to a trial before any punishment was meted out for an alleged crime. He felt the Fourteenth Amendment imposed this responsibility on the states. In fact, the state had a responsibility to protect Maples while he was in state custody. Meanwhile, Riggins argued that the Fourteenth Amendment applied to states and not to private individuals like himself. He argued that the lynching was a private action, not a state action. Judge Jones made a distinction between the equal protection and due processes clauses in the US Constitution: "Purely private actions that deny persons the equal protection of the laws may not come under the Equal Protection Clause, but the Due Process Clause is different" (Eidsmore 258). Jones continued, "When the state seeks to punish the citizen for crime, it must not only give a lawful tribunal, but it must afford the opportunity as well. Having put the accused in jail, it must keep him safely and bring him before that tribunal" (Eidsmore 258). Riggins's petition for a writ of habeas corpus was denied. Riggins appealed the case to the US Supreme Court, but the Court did not reverse Judge Jones's decision, and it did not rule on the issue of the Fourteenth Amendment due process clause.

In 1906, the Supreme Court of the United States decided *Hodges v. United States* and struck down a federal law that made it a criminal offense to make blacks desist from an employment contract. Because there was no state action, the Fourteenth Amendment did not apply. Then the next year, Judge Jones heard the case of the *United States v. Powell*. Powell had been part of the same mob as Riggins. Powell used the ruling in the Hodges case for his defense. Judge Jones then displayed remarkable courage by defending his ruling in the Riggins case with a criticism of the US Supreme Court with regard to the Hodges ruling. Nevertheless, Judge Jones upheld Powell's demurrer stating that prolonging his case would cause undue expense and inconvenience. Jones felt he had a duty to follow precedents established by the Supreme Court; his views were well ahead of those of the Supreme Court.

In 1888, Thomas Goode Jones ran against Reuben Kolb for the governor's position and was able to win in what was later called a stolen election. The Democrats were accused of stuffing the ballot boxes with thousands of ostensibly African American votes in black counties. Four years later, Jones and Kolb ran against each other once again. Kolb promised to support crop prices and promised to regulate the railroads that were imposing high fees on farms goods shipped to market via the railroad. Kolb also opposed the convict leasing system. But Jones promised to revive the state's economy by encouraging the explosive growth of Birmingham and to help wealthy plantation owners.

During Jones's tenure as governor of Alabama, historian John Craig Stewart wrote,

But aside from all the bitter conflict, the achievements of Jones' administration were substantial. The Educational Apportionment Act was passed, which provided for appropriation of educational funds to counties on a basis of school population. The Alabama School for Negro Deaf Mutes and Blind (later the Alabama Institute for Deaf and Blind). was established at Talladega. Alabama College (later Montevallo University). was founded and agricultural schools were established at Athens and Evergreen. A complete reform of the convict system was begun, and the legislature finally increased taxation, raising the tax from four mills to five mills on the dollar (Eidsmoe, 165–166).

The South was continuing along the lines of violent racial ideology that would continue for the next 100 years. Walter B. Jones wrote that his father Thomas Goode Jones used his military experience to preserve law and order in Alabama:

> He was firm in the suppression of lawlessness and frequently used the military to prevent mobs from lynching prisoners—no matter what crime was charged against them, and on the other hand, freely used the pardoning power in favor of the weak and humble who, in the passions of the times, were frequently dealt with harshly for small offenses. In May, 1894, he took personal charge of the troops and put down without bloodshed the Coal Miners' Strike in the Birmingham District and later, in July of that same year, the Debs Strike (W. B. Jones 106-107).

John Milner, a wealthy Alabama industrialist, pushed for a continuation of the convict lease system that forced African Americans to fill his mines with cheap labor. He published a pamphlet in 1890, titled *White Men of Alabama, Stand Together,* that denounced any suggestion of allowing African Americans equal political rights. Henry Cabot Lodge, Republican from Massachusetts, sponsored the "Force Bill" in the US Congress in Washington DC in the early 1890s, and this effort inflamed the racial situation even more. This bill mandated that the voting rights of African Americans be protected in the South by federal supervision of all elections, which raised the possibility of federal troops returning to the South. The election of 1892 was followed by even more actions taken against the liberties of African Americans in Alabama by the state legislature. The election campaigning encouraged more activity toward ending all political involvement by blacks and more reduction of all efforts by the Alabama state government to improve the lives of African

Americans. Candidates also mandated separate seating of the races on trains. The most critical target was public education. The state of Alabama fortified its use of government taxes for the improvement of schools for white children, but not for the schools of black children, and this tactic continued for years to come (Blackmon 102–4).

John Pace recognized the value of forced black labor, and he started the practice of providing arrested blacks to farmers who would pay him for their work. When Pace became the county sheriff, he was quickly able to round up black men for forced labor in his enterprise. He even made a deal with the county judge so that he could lease every black man sentenced to hard labor as well as any who could not pay their court costs or fines. He joined forces with Fletch Turner to include all prisoners arrested in Coosa County after signing a contract with the probate judge of that county. Their business thrived.

When Theodore Roosevelt became president following President William McKinley's assassination, he was concerned with solving the nation's political and economic problems, especially the racial divide in America. He deluded himself into thinking that all white Americans wanted to treat freed slaves fairly. He thought he could rely on all American corporations to balance their profits with the needs of the nations' workers. President T. Roosevelt spoke at the Tuskegee Institute about these issues and visited Montgomery, Alabama, in an effort to advance his agenda. Booker T. Washington encouraged black society to accommodate and acquiesce to the white demands for subservience while building their skills and acquiring an education. In 1901, as a result of President Roosevelt's relationship with Booker T. Washington, Roosevelt appointed Thomas Jones to be a federal judge for Alabama's northern and middle districts. Roosevelt wanted to reward a progressive Southerner, which is how he visualized Thomas Jones. He wanted someone who opposed lynching and someone who would stop John W. Pace and Fletch Turner.

In this capacity, Judge Jones presided over a series of cases brought by the US government that attempted to end the corrupt arrangements among certain employers who wanted to hold black citizens in peonage. Judge Jones was a delegate to the state's 1901 constitutional convention. The revised constitution that resulted from this convention governed Alabama for the next century. He tried to stop all efforts that curtailed the voting of black citizens. One issue had to do with militia service. The Standing Committee on Militia had presented a report in which they defined those eligible for the militia as "all able bodied white male inhabitants of the State, between the ages of eighteen years and forty five years."Jones urged that the word "white" be removed.

> I remember well, Mr. President, in the dark days, when the sun of the Confederacy was setting around us, while our own troops were in the trenches at Petersburg in 1865, that the Confederate Congress, under the inspiration of Robert E. Lee, passed an act authorizing the employment of Negroes in the Confederate army. The time may come in the future when we may desire to employ the Negro in the defense of this State ... We all remember, that in the Spanish war, when, for some reason, there seemed to be difficulty getting the requisite quota from Alabama, 1000 negroes volunteered, which saved 1000 white men from going ... We now have only one company of Negroes in the Alabama State troops. They were organized, I think, some twenty years ago. They have never been disbanded. The have been remarkably obedient (quoted in Eidsmore 193).

He was opposed to segregating tax funds so that only black taxes could be used to advance black education. The judge was also involved in the controversy between the state of Alabama and the railroads, especially the Louisville and Nashville Railroad. He defended the railroads and granted injunctions blocking enforcement of state regulation of the railroads (Freyer and Dixon).

Meanwhile, President Theodore Roosevelt invited Booker T. Washington to dine with him at the White House. Although black men could not be elected leaders in the United States, they could be influential. The reaction throughout the South was as expected. US

Senator Ben Tilman of South Carolina said, "Now that President Roosevelt has eaten with that nigger Booker T. Washington, we shall have to kill a thousand niggers to get them back to their places" (quoted in Blackmon 166). The governor of Georgia, Allen Candler, said, "No southerner can respect any white man who would eat with a Negro" (quoted in Blackmon 167). Mississippi politician James K. Vardaman called President Roosevelt a "little mean, coon flavored miscegenationist."

In June 1903, Judge Jones advised Attorney General Philander Knox in Washington DC, about the convict lease system. He said, "The plan is to accuse the Negro of some petty offense, and then require him, in order to escape conviction, to enter into an agreement to pay his accuser so much money, and sign a contract, under the terms of which his bondsmen can hire him out until he pays a certain sum. The Negro is made to believe he is a convict, and treated as such. It is said that thirty Negroes were in the stockade at one time." Judge Jones wanted Washington to send a special investigator (Blackmon 171). Judge Jones believed that blacks should not be mistreated in their punishment and that all citizens should receive impartial treatment by the courts. Judge Jones believed that the federal peonage statute of 1867, prohibited the peonage system that existed in Alabama.

The peonage statute declared, "The system known as peonage is abolished and forever prohibited in the territory of New Mexico, or in any other territory or state of the United States, and that it declared null and void any acts, laws, resolutions, orders, regulations, or usages in New Mexico or any other territory or state made to establish, maintain, or enforce, directly or indirectly the voluntary or involuntary service or labor of any persons or peons, in liquidation of any debt or obligation" (*Peonage Cases*, 123 F. 671, 673–75 [1903]). Judge Jones stated that the 1867 peonage statute was constitutional. The Thirteenth Amendment prohibited slavery and involuntary servitude. Finally, peonage violated the equal protection and guarantee of Article I of the 1901 Alabama constitution. Jones cited Justice Thomas Cooley: "Every one has the right to demand that he be governed by general rules, and a special statute, which, without his consent, singles his case out as one to be regulated by a different law from that which is applied in all similar cases, would not be legitimate legislation, but such an arbitrary mandates as is not within the province of free government" (Ala. Const. Art I [1901]).

In 1905, Judge Jones presented a paper "Has the Citizen of the United States in the Custody of the State's officers, upon accusation of Crime Against its Laws, any Immunity or Right which may be protected by the United States against Mob Violence?"

When a case involving peonage and convict leasing was brought to the court of Judge Jones by US Attorney Reese that involved George Crosby and his nephew, they pleaded guilty and said they did not know the law. They claimed that their imprisonment would harm their families. Federal authorities remonstrated that the official systems of leasing black convicts to private companies and individuals were indistinguishable from slavery, which still existed on some private farms. To the defendants, Judge Jones responded,

> The excuse that you did not know that you were violating the laws of the United States can have no legal weight, since every man is conclusively presumed to know the law. Ignorance of the law is not entitled to a particle of moral weight in these cases, because you are bound to know that what you did was a violation of the laws of God and of the State regardless of any law of the United States. Helpless and defenseless people who are guilty of no crime have been brought into court and by collusion with justices of the peace, who prostituted the authority of God and of this State in the administration of justice, have been deprived of their liberty, fined, forced to work and in some instances cruelly beaten. You have not only the laws of your country but that great law of honor and justice, which bids the powerful and strong not to oppress the down-trodden (quoted in Blackmon 224).

Unfortunately, despite Judge Jones's efforts to stop this involuntary servitude, the practice was flourishing in other states such as Texas, Tennessee, and Mississippi. Instead of ending this miscarriage of justice, all of these efforts seemed only to encourage a reorganization of the illegal traffic in black men. Most judicial opinions and efforts to stop this practice fell on deaf ears, and peonage continued for some time to come.

According to Douglas Blackmon in his book *Slavery by Another Name,* "What made Judge Jones more progressive than other whites, and where he differed from most white southerners, was that he believed blacks could not be brutalized in their punishment, and that the concept of impartial treatment of all citizens by the courts had to be upheld." By 1915, there were at lest 3,000 black prisoners at work in Alabama's forced-labor coal mines. After World War I was over, and thousands of black soldiers returned home thinking and hoping that the racial animosity was abating, they were disappointed to see that there were riots in South Carolina, Texas, Illinois, Arkansas, and even Washington DC, and to encounter a new wave of lynching.

6   The Scottsboro Boys and Judge James E. Horton

During the Depression years, it was not unusual to see people walking or riding trucks around looking for work. Some even hopped onto rail cars illegally without paying a fare just to get from one city to another, in search of a job and money with which they could feed their families. There were rumors of work available in Memphis, Tennessee, and several people were on the train on April 23, 1931, going from Chattanooga, Tennessee, as it traveled through Alabama, from Stevenson to Paint Rock, on its way to Memphis. There were several groups of white young men, black young men, and a few women. While the train was in Alabama, a fight broke out between four young white men and some of the black men. Apparently, one of the white men had stepped on the hand of a black man while walking on the top of a tank car in the train. When the train reached Paint Rock, a posse of 50 white men had gathered and arrested the nine black men and boys and transferred them to Scottsboro, Alabama, where they were imprisoned. The two white women, allegedly prostitutes, were also detained. Because the white women were afraid they would be charged with a violation of the Mann Act, in that they were crossing state lines for immoral purposes, they claimed that the black men had raped them. Immediately, the black men were charged with rape; it was commonly believed that no white woman in Alabama would agree to consensual sex with a black man. It did not seem to matter that no crime ever occurred. These arrests initiated the process of many trials, convictions, reversals, and retrials, more so than with any other alleged crime in American history. The white crowd that gathered in Scottsboro hoped to participate in a lynching, but Governor B. M. Miller of Alabama ordered the National Guard to protect the young men and boys.

The first trial was held approximately two weeks after the arrests, which was a step in the right direction given that a lynching otherwise was very likely. But the outcome was predetermined because there was no question among the white jury members that the defendants were guilty of rape. The nine defendants were first tried by Circuit Judge Alfred E. Hawkins in Scottsboro, with circuit solicitor H. G. Bailey prosecuting. The headlines of the local newspaper read, "All Negroes were positively identified by the girls and one white boy who was held prisoner with pistols and knives while the nine black friends committed the revolting crime." Stephen Roddy and Milo Moody were the two lawyers chosen to represent the defendants. Roddy was an uncompensated, unprepared Chattanooga real estate lawyer who had a drinking problem, and Moody, age seventy, had not tried a case in many years. Moody had been a Jackson County delegate to the 1901 constitutional convention and was described by one who knew him as a "doddering, extremely unreliable, senile individual who is losing whatever ability he once had." The trial lawyers were incompetent and agreed to try all nine defendants as a group (Carter).

Because the trials started just a few weeks after the arrests, the lawyers had no time for preparation of their cases. The prosecution felt that trying all of the defendants together might be grounds for an appeal and retrial, so they proposed that they be tried in groups of three. Furthermore, Roy Wright was only twelve years old, and his sentence would have to be different from those of the older defendants. Ruby Bates and Victoria Price were the two women involved, and their stories did not match or coincide. Victoria Price was cross-examined for no more than just a few minutes, and the two doctors who performed a physical examination on the women, Dr. R. R. Bridges and Dr. John Lynch, were not cross-examined at all.

Of the defendants, Andy Wright, Willie Roberson, Charles Weems, Ozie Powell, Olen Montgomery, and Eugene Williams denied raping the women or, in fact, even seeing the women. But the three others, after beatings and threats, testified that all of the black men had raped the two white women. Because the defense attorneys did not give a closing argument, the state's case was described as being perfect. The court then announced the guilty verdicts after the first trial, when the second trial was about to commence. Eight of the nine boys were sentenced to death, but the prosecution asked for only a life sentence for the twelve-year-old boy.

The NAACP (National Association for the Advancement of Colored People). did not rush to get involved because they suspected that the boys were guilty and that this might hinder their effectiveness in advancing civil rights. But the Communist Party saw this as a possible propaganda opportunity and immediately volunteered to defend the so-called Scottsboro boys for appeal trials. Thus, through the International Labor Defense (ILD)., they called this a "murderous frame-up." Later, the NAACP realized that this indeed was a frame-up, and so they hired Clarence Darrow to defend the accused in Alabama. Unfortunately for the Scottsboro Boys, they elected to have the Communist Party defend them, not realizing that the Communists were treated no better in the South than a gang of black alleged rapists. In January 1932, the Alabama Supreme Court by a 6–1 vote affirmed all but one of the sentences. At the foundation of the Southern response was the belief that the black race was inferior to the white race and that the blacks had to be controlled.

The Scottsboro boys spent the two years between the first trial and the second trial at the Kilby prison in Montgomery, Alabama. The case went to the Alabama Supreme Court, which affirmed all convictions and scheduled the executions. The case then was appealed to the United States Supreme Court, which reversed all of the previous decisions and ordered another trial. The prisoners were confined to a tiny cell and could hear the sounds of others being electrocuted. Once a week, they were walked to a shower, but otherwise they stayed confined to their cells. As the trial date approached, they were transferred in March 1933 to another prison in Decatur, Alabama, a prison that had been condemned for white prisoners.

The second trial of Haywood Patterson began March 30, 1933, in Decatur, Alabama, in the courtroom of Judge James Horton. Thomas Knight was to be the prosecutor in the retrials. Samuel Leibowitz was the lead attorney representing the Scottsboro boys. Although he was rumored to be a Communist because he was Jewish, he had impeccable credentials and had absolutely no connection with the Communist Party. Leibowitz tried to cancel the trial altogether given that black citizens were not allowed to serve on the jury, and he criticized Thomas Knight for calling the defendants by their first names. Needless to say, a Northern Jewish lawyer coming to Alabama and attacking the way things were done there did not go over well.

On April 3, 1933, the prostitute Victoria Price was called to the stand, and she said that she had stayed at Callie Brochie's boarding house in Chattanooga prior to boarding the train, but the evidence showed there was no such boarding house in Chattanooga. She told of boarding the train looking for work, discussed the interracial fight on the train, and related the details of a gang rape in which Haywood Patterson participated. She did admit that she was an adulterer and a prostitute and that she had had sex with Jack Tiller in the Huntsville freight yard two days before the alleged rape. Jack Tiller was only involved as he happened to be one of Victoria Price's prostitution clients. In fact, it was either his semen or that of Orville Gilley that was found in her vagina. She showed no contrition and had no bruises or injuries of any kind. She thought the posse in Paint Rock was coming after her because she had violated the Mann Act. She was using these groundless accusations to divert attention away from her own problems, and she blamed a poor memory for not recalling any details of the events. But she did remember that when one of the alleged rapists pulled "his thing out," he told her she would have a black baby. The only eyewitness to the events supposedly was Ory

Dobbins. He said he saw the black defendants grab the two women and then jump from the train. He was asked how he knew they were women given that he was so far away. He replied that the women were wearing dresses. In reality, the women were wearing men's overalls.

Leibowitz called witnesses to discredit Victoria Price and to show that she was a liar. Chattanooga resident Dallas Ramsey testified that he had seen Victoria Price at the "hobo jungle," but Price said she had never been there. Lester Carter, a twenty-three-year-old traveling companion to the two women, testified that both he and Jack Tiller had had sex with the two women in the Huntsville hobo jungle the night before the alleged rape. He had sex with Ruby Bates, and his companion had sex with Victoria Price. When the fighting broke out on the train, some of the white boys jumped off the train.Six of the defendants said that they were suffering from a venereal disease and were too weak to have raped anyone, much less to jump off a moving train.

Knight asked Haywood Patterson whether he was tried in Scottsboro, and he answered, "I was framed in Scottsboro."

The jurors were asked by the prosecuting attorney Knight "whether justice in this case is going to be bought and sold with Jew money from New York." Leibowitz immediately asked for a new trial, but Judge Horton denied the request. Leibowitz called the accusations of Price a "foul contemptible, outrageous lie." He closed with the Lord's Prayer and asked the jury to either acquit the defendants or give them the chair. The jury deliberated for five minutes and found Patterson guilty and sentenced him to death. Ruby Bates returned east with Leibowitz and attended rallies for the Scottsboro boys and made the case for them. While she was in New York city, she met with Rev. Harry Emerson Fosdick of that city and he persuaded her to return to Alabama and to tell the truth. So toward the end of the trial, she recanted.

On June 22, 1933, Judge James Horton convened court in his hometown of Athens, Alabama, to hear yet another trial. By this time, Horton was convinced that Victoria Price was lying. Her story had many inconsistencies and was not corroborated by the medical evidence or other witnesses. Dr. John Lynch, who also had examined the women, said that he was convinced the women were lying and told them so, only to have them laugh at him. But Dr. Lynch was just recently out of medical school and was trying to build a practice in the community. If word leaked out that he thought the women were lying, he would have to build a practice elsewhere. Judge Horton sympathized with Dr. Lynch given that he himself was up for reelection the next year and was warned that if he set the decision aside, he would be committing political suicide. But Judge Horton, who believed one should "let justice be done, though the heavens may fail," surprised everyone by setting aside the verdict and showing great courage in ordering a new trial. Judge Horton said that history had taught that women of the character shown in the trial do make false accusations of rape upon the slightest provocation. On June 22, 1933, Judge Horton stated that the evidence favored the defendant and that he did not believe the boys were guilty. He then ordered still another trial. The Alabama Supreme Court removed Judge Horton from the case and appointed Judge Washington Callahan to the case. As expected, Judge Horton, who had run unopposed in the previous election, lost his judgeship in the next election. Judge William Callahan was named to preside at the next trial for Haywood Patterson, scheduled to begin November, 1933.

Judge William Callahan would not have his name listed in perpetuity as one of those who made courageous decisions, but rather should be listed as a judge who did not have any judicial principles. His goal was to get the case settled and to get these boys off the front pages of all the newspapers. He made it difficult for the journalists to cover the trials and did not provide any protection for the lawyers who were defending the Scottsboro boys. Besides acting more like a prosecutor than a judge, he set a time limit of three days, maximum, for any one trial. He supported the prosecution and never sustained the objections of the lawyers for the defense. None of the seven white boys were put on the stand. He did not allow any discussion of Victoria's sex history, nor would he allow any intimation that she may have had sex with someone other than the Scottsboro boys.

One of the stars at the third trial for Haywood Patterson was Mr. Orville Gilley. His account supported that of Victoria Price in many ways, but it did surface that the lawyer for the prosecution had sent money to both his mother and him ahead of the trial. Victoria Price said that after the last man raped her, someone put her overalls back on when the posse met them at Paint Rock. An hour afterward, Dr. Bridges and Dr. Lynch examined her, and they did not find any lacerations or bruises, nor did she have any rapid breathing or a rapid pulse. In fact, the spermatozoa found in her vagina were no longer alive. The two doctors did not find any evidence of vaginal bleeding. As noted previously, there was evidence that the women had spent the night at the hobo dive and that they had had sexual intercourse with men there, and there was no evidence that the women had had sex with any of the black defendants. There was no evidence that any of the black men had wet or damp spots on their clothes. The testimony that Victoria Price gave was contradictory and evasive. In fact, as noted earlier, the evidence indicated that the two women had had sexual intercourse with Lester Carter and Jack Tiller while in jail in Huntsville. As expected Haywood Patterson was sentenced to death again. Immediately after his trial, Clarence Norris was tried and he too was found guilty. Judge Callahan agreed to postpone any further trials for the others charged with rape until the appeals process for the first two defendants had run its course.

On February 15, 1935, the US Supreme Court heard arguments in the Haywood Patterson and the Clarence Norwood cases. Mr. Leibowitz, the lawyer for the Scottsboro boys, argued that because Alabama excluded blacks from jury selection, which was a violation of the equal protection clause in the US Constitution, the verdicts should be overturned. Leibowitz argued that some names of African Americans had been forged onto the jury roles after the second trial had begun, and Chief Justice Evans Hughes asked whether he could prove this. Leibowitz produced a page from the jury rolls with a magnifying glass, and the justices examined the evidence. Six weeks later, the Supreme Court ordered still another trial for the two defendants. The Supreme Court said,

> We find to warrant for a conclusion that the names of any of the Negroes as to whom this testimony was given, or of another Negro, were placed on the jury rolls. No such names were identified. The evidence that for many years no Negro has been called for jury service itself tended to show the absence of the names of Negroes from the jury rolls, and the state made no effort to prove their presence. For this long continued, unvarying and wholesale exclusion of Negroes from jury service we find no justification consistent with the constitutional mandate (Norris v. Alabama, 55s. ct, 294 U.S. 587, No. 534, 1935).

But Patterson was once again found to be guilty of rape January 23, 1936. The jury sentenced him to seventy-five years in prison, which was the first time a black man was not given the death sentence in Alabama after being convicted of raping a white woman.

Throughout, this case had unusual moments. Apparently, while officials were transporting the other Scottsboro boys to a Birmingham jail during the Patterson trial, Ozie Powell, who was handcuffed in the rear of the car, extracted a penknife from his pocket and cut the neck of the deputy sheriff. The sheriff stopped the car and shot Powell in the head. Even though Powell survived, according to Clarence Norris, he was never the same again.

Judge Callahan tried to speed the trials of the remaining Scottsboro boys because of the heat. By 1937, seven of the Scottsboro boys had been held in jail for over six years without a trial. After a two-day trial, the jury rendered a death sentence for Clarence Norris on July 15, 1937. Andy Wright was sentenced to ninety-nine years in prison. Charlie Weem was sentenced to seventy-five years in prison. The jury dropped the rape charges against Ozie Powell because he pleaded guilty to assaulting a deputy. The prosecution announced that they were dropping the charges against the four remaining defendants. Roy Wright and Eugene Williams were twelve and thirteen years old at the time of their arrests, and it was felt that perhaps they were not guilty of rape.

Whether through parole, escape, or pardon, all of the Scottsboro boys eventually got out of Alabama. Charles Weems was paroled in 1943. Ozie Powell and Clarence Norris were pardoned in 1946. Andy Wright, who had been convicted of rape and sentenced to 99 years, was finally released in 1950 by paroling him to New York and was the last to leave Alabama. Haywood Patterson made a dramatic escape in 1948, and while he was a fugitive, he wrote a book titled *Scottsboro Boys,* which was published in 1950. Patterson was arrested in Michigan for killing a man in a bar fight and he was convicted of manslaughter in December 1950 and was sentenced to six to fifteen years in prison. He died in the Michigan prison August 24, 1952, after serving one year. Governor G. Mennen Williams refused to extradite him back to Alabama.

Governor George Wallace officially pardoned Clarence Norris who then returned to Alabama to receive and accept the pardon in October 1976.

7   Judge Frank M. Johnson Jr.

President Dwight Eisenhower named Judge Frank Johnson a federal judge in 1955. During his forty years as a federal judge of the Eleventh US Circuit Court of Appeals, his tenure coincided with the most contentious period in twentieth-century legal history. Even today as we seek replacements for retiring members of the US Supreme Court, we hear arguments that judges should not be judicial activists, but should interpret the Constitution as it was written. Judge Johnson felt that the Constitution's strength was its flexibility and that it needed to be changed to reflect the needs of society. Although the people in Alabama were very conscious of their rights, they were concerned with the role of the federal judiciary, the growing policy-making role of the federal government, and the effect of both on their daily lives. This tension influenced many of the judicial decisions made by Alabama's Judge Frank Johnson. He ruled that the segregation employed by the Montgomery bus system was unconstitutional. He also ensured that the march from Selma to Montgomery was approved. He desegregated public schools and colleges, parks, libraries, train and bus depots, airports, restaurants, restrooms, and the Alabama State Police. He sent the killers of civil rights worker Viola Liuzzo to jail. He restrained attacks on Freedom Riders and mandated changes for the improvement of Alabama prisons. Governor George Wallace backed down from every confrontation with Judge Frank Johnson. In the *Frontiero v. Laird* (1972). case, he rendered a dissenting opinion. This case dealt with the issue of whether the Army could discriminate against a woman army officer and refuse to pay spousal benefits. Later, the Supreme Court agreed with Judge Johnson that the Army's rule was unconstitutional.

There was one issue on which no one seemed to take any action. Governor Lurleen Wallace witnessed the unacceptable conditions in Alabama's mental institutions but did not take any effective action to remedy the situation. In the 1970s a class action lawsuit was filed on behalf of Ricky Wyatt, who was a patient at Bryce Hospital. The suit alleged that the state's underfunding had led to staff cuts and poor treatment for the inmates at the three state mental hospitals, Bryce, Searcy, and Partlow. There is no doubt that the hospitals were overcrowded, filthy, and understaffed. The patients were chained to their beds and were allowed to stay in their own waste. No more than fifty cents a day was spent on the food for the patients, and there was only one physician for more than 2,200 patients. Dr. Stone Stickney was the new commissioner of mental health, and he wanted to decentralize the mental health hospital system. He also wanted to have many local hospitals involved so that patients' families could participate in their care, but the state did not have the money for such a revision in the care of the mentally ill. In fact, the state was forced to terminate ninety-nine employees in 1970. Several officials had witnessed that patients slept on the floor, that the plumbing in the shower stalls did not work, and that human feces were caked on the toilets and the bathroom walls. They also knew that the patients had not been bathed in weeks and that the temperatures in the rooms were often at 100 degrees.

Judge Frank Johnson presided at the court that was to hear the arguments of this case, and Middle District US Attorney Ira DeMint presented the case for the Justice Department. In 1971 in this case, Judge Johnson ruled that the patients had a constitutional right to receive adequate treatment and so ordered the state of Alabama to develop and present a plan within six months to rectify this abhorrent situation. Unfortunately, the state of Alabama fought the order and delayed implementation of any plan. So in 1972, Judge Johnson issued an order for the immediate employment of three hundred aides and professional staff. By doing this, he established that mental patients do have constitutional rights to have at least the minimum standard of care. The *Wyatt v. Stickney* case went to the Supreme Court, where the verdict was upheld, which encouraged other states to follow and implement reform. In part as a result of this case, other agencies sought social reform. Some of these included the Children First Foundation, Voices for Alabama's Children, the Alabama Poverty Project, Alabama Arise, and Healthy Alabama 2000. The Children First Foundation benefited the most, with the infant mortality rate dropping dramatically in Alabama. Although these reform efforts involved academic offices, law offices, and Sunday school classrooms, they did not involve the Alabama state legislature.

Years before the mental health case, on December 1, 1955, Rosa Parks was riding on the Cleveland Avenue bus. When she refused to give up her seat to a white man and move to the back of the bus, the police were summoned in front of the Empire Theater on Montgomery Street. Ms. Parks was taken to jail, fingerprinted, and given fifty-six days of hard labor, which was put on hold until another similar case was also resolved. Then on February 1, 1956, Claudette Colvin was arrested for not sitting in the colored section of the bus (i.e., the back of the bus). as well. A suit was filed challenging the legality of such a rule in what was known as the *Browder v. Gayle* case. Ms. Browder was a black woman made to stand on the bus, and Gayle was the mayor of Montgomery. When the case came before Judge Johnson, he felt that *Brown v. Topeka Department of Education* (1954). overruled the *Plessy v. Ferguson* (1896). case and that separate but equal was no longer the law of the land. He felt that this applied not only to public education but also to other areas, including public transportation.

Judge Frank Johnson said,

> As far as I was concerned, it wasn't a difficult case to decide. There were no conflicting constitutional questions at issue. The long and short of it was that there was a state law that said Negroes—simply because they were Negroes— had to ride in the back of the bus and had been extended to

say they had to get up when white folks wanted their seat. Now [Montgomery County Circuit] Judge Walter Jones had asked the question, "Where in the Constitution is there one word, one sentence, one paragraph" that says you couldn't segregate folks in public transportation? My question was "Where in the Constitution is there anything that says you can segregate them?" It just isn't there. To the contrary, it specifically says you can't abridge the freedoms of the individual. The boycott case was a simple case of legal and human rights being denied (quoted in Sikora 46–47).

Judge Rives joined Judge Johnson on this case, and they issued opinions that in effect said that due process and equal protection under the law, as provided for under the Fourteenth Amendment of the US Constitution of the United States, had been violated by Alabama law. At that time in Alabama, black people could not serve on juries, could not run for political office, and were excluded from public accommodations. Not only could black people not attend public schools with white children; they also were expected to ride in the back of the bus and use separate restrooms and water fountains. And on November 13, 1956, the US Supreme Court upheld the June 5 decision of Judge Rives and Judge Johnson, which banned segregation on the Montgomery city buses.

Judge Frank Johnson said, "As long as there are people, there will be discrimination of some type. Prejudice doesn't depend entirely on race, it's not always a black-and-white issue. It can be just as vicious and hateful among different ethnic or religious groups" (quoted in Sikora 56).

Judge Johnson also ruled on voting rights in Macon, Bullock, Barbour, and Montgomery counties and put the ballot back into the hands of black people, but the press initially overlooked this because there were no demonstrations or marches on this issue.

The Freedom Riders came to Alabama to protest the Jim Crow laws and segregation, and felt that this demonstration would bring national attention to the racial problem. Floyd Mann, Director of the Alabama Department of Public Safety, knew that the bus carrying the students from the north, who were protesting the Alabama segregation system, was en route from Birmingham to Montgomery. He knew that the reception these students on the bus had received in Anniston was only a prelude to what they would encounter in Montgomery. Accordingly, he did advise the director of the Montgomery police department, L. B. Sullivan, and Chief Ruppenthal that they should take the necessary precautions. Director Floyd Mann had sixteen patrol cars and one airplane accompany the bus to Montgomery in order to reduce the chances of violence.

Judge Frank Johnson sympathized with the Freedom Riders but felt they were fighting for their cause in the wrong way. He also felt they should have contacted the authorities in Anniston and should not have pushed the issue by riding first to Birmingham and then on to the Montgomery bus station where they were viciously beaten by a mob. Judge Johnson enjoined the Ku Klux Klan (KKK) from interfering with the travel of the bus passengers and committing acts of violence. He also filed an injunction aimed at the police officials of the Montgomery police department. Finally, the court entered a ruling November, 1961, that stopped discrimination at all levels of interstate transportation, and this might have happened without all of the violence at the Montgomery bus station (Sikora 144).

Judge Frank Johnson had the following to say about the freedom riders:

> Some northern newspapers were dismayed that I included the freedom riders in my restraining order. And the reason I did is that I felt they went about pursuing their rights in the wrong way. When they ran into trouble in Anniston—their first stop in Alabama—they should have quit and come to the courts. That's why we have courts. But they did not do that. Instead, they kept on and it not only created strife, it also interfered with the other passengers who were riding buses. It impeded the normal flow of interstate commerce.

They should have come to the courts and presented their grievances.

Now what makes the freedom riders different from the blacks who took part in the bus boycott in Montgomery is that the boycott was a negative protest, so to speak. People just quit riding buses. But they did not bother anyone else; did not interfere with others riding them (quoted in Sikora 146).

Although there had been numerous attempts by African Americans to enroll their children in schools that were all-white at the time, these efforts were frequently met with white resistance and violence. Rev. Fred Shuttlesworth and Rev. J. S. Phifer tried to enroll four black children in white schools in Birmingham September 11, 1957, only to be confronted with a gang of thirty white men with brass knuckles, chains, and clubs. Six years later, Mr. and Mrs. Detroit Lee of Tuskegee filed suit so that their son Anthony and other black children could enter the Tuskegee High School. On July 22, 1963, Judge Frank Johnson ordered that the Macon County School Board allow black students to enter all of the previously white schools. This case, *Lee v. Macon,* was the central battle of school desegregation in Alabama. Governor George Wallace stood in the schoolhouse door at the University of Alabama trying to keep the state university from being integrated in June 1963. Governor Wallace also sent some of his supporters to various schools throughout Alabama in an effort to frustrate the integration process. The US Justice Department asked Judge Frank Johnson to declare a statewide integration order, but Judge Johnson said he did not have that authority. Thus, the Justice Department contacted other district judges and convened a panel in Montgomery to discuss and rectify the situation. This body issued a restraining order that prevented Governor Wallace and his state troopers from interfering with the integration of schools in Tuskegee, Mobile, and Birmingham. Then Governor Wallace tried to replace his troopers with the Alabama National Guard, but President Kennedy federalized these Guard troops who helped integrate the public schools. As if all of this was not incendiary enough, there was a bombing of the Sixteenth Street Baptist Church in Birmingham,

Alabama, on September 15, 1963, which killed four young black girls while they were attending Sunday school.

From time to time, thugs at various schools attempted to frustrate desegregation of the public schools in Alabama, but desegregation became a reality throughout the state. The US Fourth Circuit Court of Appeals in Richmond interpreted *Brown v. Board of Education* as saying that a school system could not prevent black children from entering schools because of their color. But the US Fifth Circuit in New Orleans said that *Brown v. Board of Education* went further and called for an affirmative effort to bring black students into historically all-white schools. In March 1967, Judge Johnson, with Judge Rives and US District Judge Hobart Grooms, issued a statewide desegregation order that applied to all school systems except for a few in Huntsville, Alabama, where the schools were integrating on their own. Justice Ed Livingston, Chief Justice of Alabama Supreme Court; Governor Lurleen Wallace; and the state's superintendent of education, Austin Meadows, denounced this action by Judges Johnson, Rives, and Grooms. On the night of April 25, 1967, a bomb exploded at the home of Judge Johnson's mother, who fortunately was not injured. The perpetrators of this crime had mistakenly thought the house was Judge Johnson's.

Judge Frank Johnson said "The Civil Rights Movement was a social and legal revolution that shook the nation to its core. It was a drive by blacks to obtain equal rights and civil rights. It was a massive effort for equal rights and equally massive effort against equal rights, for the white reaction to it was a deep-seated racial fear. White people perceived it as an attack on the social order, on the political order, and the economic order—which were the same emotions that caused the Civil War" (Sikora p.182).

"Then," Sikora continues, "it was the abolition of slavery; in the 20th century it was the abolition of segregation and the hue and cry was just as emotional. We can all utter a prayer of thanks that the battle to end segregation did not result in as much bloodshed as the effort to abolish slavery" (182).

One of the more memorable and important civil rights efforts was the march from Selma to Montgomery in 1965. How did this come about? Martin Luther King Jr. came to Selma on January 2, 1965. Approximately two weeks later, Reverend King started leading marching demonstrations; these continued for several weeks. Sheriff Clark would wait each day at the Dallas County Courthouse and would arrest some of the black marchers each day. He filled up the local jails and even opened a dilapidated old prison, where he forced many young black marchers using cattle prods. These marches continued when, not too far away, Colonel Al Lingo, the director of public safety in Alabama, urged his state troopers to actually attack a group of black men as they were emerging from a church meeting. In fact, a woodcutter named Jimmie Jackson was shot and killed during one of these demonstrations. This prompted Martin Luther King to organize a march to Montgomery to petition Governor Wallace concerning police brutality and the denial of voting rights. But as expected, Governor Wallace issued an order barring a march from Selma to Montgomery and dispatched 200 state troopers on the south side of the Edmund Pettus Bridge, which crosses the Alabama River. When 600 marching black citizens tried to cross the bridge, the state troopers attacked them with clubs, whips, and tear gas canisters. The attorneys for the African Americans seeking their civil rights then appeared at the federal building in Montgomery requesting an injunction against Governor Wallace, Sheriff Clark, and Director Al Lingo.

Judge Frank Johnson issued two orders: (1) an order directed at the state troopers, Governor Wallace, Sheriff Clark, and Director Al Lingo enjoining them from interfering with peaceful demonstrations and (2) an order prohibiting King's followers from attempting any more marches to Montgomery until a hearing could be held on March 11, 1965. President Lyndon Johnson sent former Florida governor Leroy Collins to Selma to act an arbitrator between the two opposing sides; Governor Collins was the head of the Justice Department's Community Relations Service.

On March 9, 1965, approximately 2000 African Americans followed Martin Luther King in Selma toward the Pettus bridge crossing the Alabama river. A US marshal stopped them before they reached the bridge, read to them Judge Frank Johnson's orders that prohibited marches, and then stepped aside. When Colonel Al Lingo subsequently stopped them, Reverend King asked for permission to pray. Lingo said they could pray, and so the marchers went back to the Brown Chapel in Selma.

Judge Frank Johnson saw this as a kabuki play performance and felt that as long as there were courts, there was no need for demonstrations and marches. But the law did say there could be demonstrations as long as they were peaceful. So Judge Frank Johnson issued the order that gave the black marchers the relief they sought, in that they could march from Selma to Montgomery on certain days, two abreast, on the left side of the road. He specifically ordered Wallace, Lingo, and Clark not to do anything to impede the march, and he had assurances from Nicholas Katzenback, the US attorney general, that President Johnson backed him up and would provide security for the marchers if the state of Alabama did not do so. Judge Johnson said,

> As I watched those people—and some were mere children—I was absolutely convinced that I had been right. I had never watched a march of demonstration before, but there was something special about the Selma- to -Montgomery march. I think the people demonstrated something about democracy; that it can never be taken for granted; they also showed that there is a way in this system to gain human rights. They had followed the channel prescribed within the framework of the law. I think the march decision also showed some black people that valid complaints can be addressed within the system, according to the Constitution, and can be addressed without resorting to violence (quoted in Sikora 222).

Although the march from Selma to Montgomery had been relatively peaceful, it was what happened afterward that caused concern. After the march, there were shuttles, cars, and buses taking people back to Selma. One of those involved in the shuttle service was Mrs. Viola Gregg Liuzzo, a white housewife from Detroit, Michigan. She too was looking for a ride back to Selma, and someone gave her the keys to a car in which she would drive Leroy Morton and others back to Selma. After driving one carload of marchers back to the Brown Chapel in Selma, she turned around to return to Montgomery to get others. But after she crossed the Alabama River at the Pettus Bridge, a car began to pursue her. The car stayed behind her as she passed Craig Air Force Base and entered Lowndes County. Then the pursuing car started passing her car, and shots were fired that hit Mrs. Liuzzo in the head, bringing her car to a halt in a ditch. The next day, President Johnson announced that the FBI had arrested four Klansmen. Eugene Thomas, William Orville Eaton, Collie Leroy Wilkins, and Gary Thomas Rowe, all from the Birmingham area, were charged with murder by the state of Alabama and were charged with a violation of civil rights by the federal government.

Wilkins was the first to face a murder charge in Hayneville, Alabama, in Lowndes County. Many wondered whether an all-white jury would find this white man guilty of murder. Gary Rowe was an undercover FBI agent, and his detailed testimony was pivotal. Even so, after ten days, the jury could not make a decision, and a mistrial was declared. A second trial was scheduled in October 1965, but it was postponed until November while federal charges were pursued. Judge Frank Johnson presided, and Deputy Attorney General John Doar headed the prosecution. After a long trial, which almost ended in a mistrial, the jury returned a guilty verdict. Judge Johnson sentenced the three men to ten years each, which was the maximum authorized by statue. The Court of Appeals and the United States Supreme Court turned down appeals. Change had come to Alabama. No longer could the KKK impose its will of terror without being challenged. In fact, two years later in Mississippi, members of the Klan were brought before a federal jury on charges arising from the deaths of three civil rights workers in 1964. All of these cases broke the power of the KKK in the South.

In August 1965, about five months after Judge Johnson heard the case relating to the Selma to Montgomery march, the US Congress passed the Voting Rights Act. This allowed thousands of black citizens in the South the right to vote, and a great deal of this act contained measures that Judge Frank Johnson had written in 1961, in the voting case in Macon county. The law required the registrars to pass black applications if they were on a par with the least qualified white applicants. The law prohibited arbitrary testing and difficult exams (Sikora 224).

Although the Southern states violated the civil rights of their black citizens, there was even more discrimination by the US government. In 1932, the US Public Health Service began a study on a group of 625 black men who lived in Macon County, Alabama. The study was designed to study the progression of syphilis in a group of black men (Washington 157–85). Apparently, some felt that the progression of syphilis in black men was different than in white men. The plan was to withhold treatment from a group of infected black men and then study the outcome. The Public Health Service did not level with the men and led them to believe that in fact they were being treated for syphilis. Autopsies were scheduled for those who died, ostensibly to study the differences in the syphilis effects on the brain and the cardiovascular systems. Because the prevailing opinion was that the brains of black men were underdeveloped, it was assumed that syphilis would affect and damage their cardiovascular system and spare their immature brains. Some of the participants with syphilis were treated, and some were not treated at all. A great deal of attention was paid to this experiment so that the participants did not inadvertently receive treatment from some well meaning provider. This group was so well monitored that most did not receive any treatment at all. In fact, when World War II broke out, the group involved in the Tuskegee syphilis study were excluded from military service for fear that a military doctor would render effective treatment to these men when the Public Health Service did not want any treatment rendered to this group. The Public Health Service was concerned that effective treatment with penicillin would invalidate their study, and it spread the fiction that "these men still regard hospitals and medicine with suspicion and prefer an occasional dose of time-honored herbs and tonics to modern drugs" (Brandt 26). Thirty men did circumvent the study policy and were able to get penicillin treatment.

Even though penicillin was found to treat and cure this disease, the experiment continued for 40 years without any of the proven therapy rendered to the untreated group. The progress of this study group was reported at the American Medical Association meeting in 1936. Not until 1972 did the media learn of this injustice. Montgomery attorney Fred Gray filed a suit in the US district court and named the US government as the defendant. The case was filed on behalf of Charlie Pollard from Notasulga, who said, "I did not know until recently that I was involved in an experiment of untreated syphilis in Negro males. The Federal doctors who came and carried out this experiment in Tuskegee never told me that I was part of an experiment. I was led to believe by the Federal government personnel who conducted the study that I was receiving adequate medical care and attention. I was never told by anyone conducting the study about the effects of untreated syphilis nor was I instructed as to precautions to take for syphilis" (quoted in Sikora 259).

The lawyers for the government objected to handling this case as a class action, but Judge Frank Johnson said that this clearly was a class action case. The hearings and motions went on for a year, and the government offered the victims lifetime medical care. Mr. Fred Gray rejected this offer and said he was concerned that such a settlement would preclude damage awards. Eventually, the government agreed with Mr. Fred Gray that a class of black men had been wronged. The consent order provided $37,000 for the living syphilitics, $15,000 for the heirs of the deceased syphilitics, and $5,000 for the heirs of the deceased controls. In all, the federal government paid $8,446,000, which Judge Johnson ordered to be deposited in three banks, each paying 5 1/2 percent interest while the hundreds of claims could be sorted out. The case file stayed open for thirteen years.

As this is being written, President Obama has nominated his second judge to serve on the US Supreme Court. As has been the case since at least the time of World War II, critics are once again charging that federal judges and the Supreme Court have exercised and employed unwarranted judicial activism that interferes with the traditional judicial independence and constitutional discretion that Americans have grown used to seeing. The other side argues that judicial intervention has continued to be a necessary adjunct because the federal and state governments have failed to fulfill their duties to protect the citizens. Witness the present controversies on the constitutionality of the recently passed health care bill, which mandates that all citizens purchase health insurance or suffer the consequences. Also, Arizona has taken action to protect its citizens from undocumented immigrants who enter the United States and commit crimes against American citizens, and the federal government has refused to secure the borders. Thus, there is tension between those who want to maintain the status quo and those who want the government to respond to changes in our society.

Few judges in American and Alabama history have confronted this tension more directly than Judge Frank Johnson, who successfully defended civil rights and liberties. He overcame resistance from segregationist obstructionism and from the state government leaders who did not meet their responsibilities. He made a remarkable contribution to the civil rights revolution in Alabama, and this was consistent with the liberal views of the Supreme Court of the United States. Yet for all the respect that the citizens of Alabama had for a federal judge, there was a certain amount of tension concerning that fact that he was appointed rather than elected. This activist judge was a proponent of democracy. Still, opponents felt that Judge Johnson made law based on his personality and personal attitude rather than relying on legal canons and legal precedents. Others argued that a strong personality was a requisite for judicial independence and for a judge to defend the civil rights of all citizens (Freyer and Dixon 217–18).

Whether or not the judicial court's role in the Montgomery bus boycott and the Selma-to-Montgomery march was independent, there can be no doubt that Judge Johnson's decisions in these cases were pivotal and heroic. Much of the violence that occurred in Alabama was due to the Southern state leaders, and it was in part due to federal government leaders as well. Alabama officials were touting "states' rights" while the federal officials were content to leave these issues to be settled by local authorities. Governor Wallace actually thrived on blaming the federal government and "outside agitators" for all of the problems and violence in Alabama, and he made this politically profitable. In fact, Wallace's primary target was Judge Frank Johnson, whose judicial actions hastened the end of segregation in Alabama. Many scholars have opined about the extent to which Judge Johnson's origins and early career may have influenced him when he made these important and far-reaching decisions.

Most everyone's future is to some extent influenced by his or her past, and Judge Johnson was no exception. He grew up in the northwestern part of Alabama in Winston County, which was by and large Republican. Historically, this area was not a strong supporter of secession from the United States during the Civil War. But there were many in Winston County who believed in secession from the state of Alabama. After a meeting at Looney's Tavern, they passed a resolution for the "Free State of Winston":

> We think our neighbors in the South made a mistake when they bolted. ... however, we do not desire to see our neighbors in the South mistreated, and, therefore, we are not going to take up arms against them; but on the other hand, we are not going to shoot at the flag of our fathers, Old Glory, the flag of Washington, Jefferson, and Jackson. Therefore, we ask that the Confederacy on the one hand, and the Union on the other, leave us alone, unmolested, that we may work out our political and financial destiny here in the hills and mountains of Northwest Alabama. (quoted in Sikora 60–61; see also Jenkins and Stauffer).

Some of Johnson's ancestors fought on the Union side during the war. As a result, the community experience instilled in him values such as independence, self-reliance, integrity, and personal courage, as well as a sense of fairness in dealing with race and religion. Rather than argue their positions in a court of law, his neighbors relied on the opinion of their elders to settle disputes. Johnson's father was elected as the probate judge in Winston County and was the only Republican to serve in the Alabama legislature during the 1940s. Perhaps Judge Frank Johnson's experience in the military service dealing with criminal affairs and his experience in the private practice of law prepared him for public service.

While Johnson was living in Winston County, which was relatively isolated, the Illinois Central Railroad was the main source of transportation to the area. Many African Americans and whites worked on the railroad together and were able to make a good living. As a child, Frank Johnson played with black children and was not taught to hate those who were different. Racism was not promulgated in his town. He was home-schooled long before the practice became popular in America, but in the process, he was taught that education was paramount to success in life, as was respect for the law. Growing up in his family's household, Frank Johnson learned firsthand from his father, who again was a probate judge, fundamental fairness, and he was aware of racial injustice. As a youngster, Johnson worked for a surveyor's road crew. He saw how the white guards mistreated the black convicts who also did this type of work. If the black convicts tried to escape or just disobeyed an order, a guard would employ his bullwhip and beat the black convicts unmercifully. Johnson found the sight of one human being whipping another human being with a bullwhip nauseating. Johnson said, "I have some strong, basic religious beliefs. Doing what's right and wrong to me is a religious belief. And doing what's fair instead of unfair to a fellow human being is a religious standard" (quoted in Freyer and Dixon 222). Judge Frank Johnson once said, "I never liked the term 'reverse discrimination' because it means nothing. There is no such thing as reverse discrimination, just as there is no such thing as reverse murder, or reverse robbery. It's merely something the news media conjured up to mean blacks that discriminate against whites. But there is just plain old discrimination. It can be carried out by whites, it can be carried out by blacks, or any other race or group" (quoted in Sikora 260).

Judge Johnson's educational background strengthened his administrative and managerial skills. After graduating from the Winston County public schools and the Gulf Coast Military Academy, he attended Birmingham Southern prior to going to the University of Alabama. Johnson's view was that each individual has to take responsibility for his achievements and his failures. In addition, each individual has to know his own strengths and weaknesses. Thus, his education and intellectual acuity along with life experiences helped Johnson interpret the constitutional law with regard to race relations. Growing up with black children, working on the railroad with African Americans, and seeing the mistreatment of black convicts while working on the surveyor's road crew all shaped his attitude that racial segregation was wrong. Even as a law student, Johnson felt that the Dred Scott case of 1857, was scandalous in that it approved of slavery. He also felt that the *Plessy v. Ferguson* (1896)., which approved of the separate but equal way of life, was a bad decision, but he admired Justice John Marshall Harlan's lone dissent. He saw what judicial courage really was.

As of this writing, many Americans, particularly Republicans, feel that President Obama's liberalism constitutes an unconstitutional aggrandizement of the executive power. Judge Frank Johnson had the same opinion of the many acts that President Roosevelt pushed through Congress during his four terms as president. But Judge Johnson supported the Works Progress Administration (WPA). and other New Deal programs that helped the people of Alabama. While in college, he befriended George Wallace, who would eventually be the governor of Alabama and Johnson's adversary and antagonist.

Frank Johnson was also influenced by his wartime experiences, during which he was awarded the Bronze Star and a Purple Heart. He was twice wounded while serving in France and Germany. While in England serving as a legal officer, he represented the defendants in one of the most publicized trials in military history. Nine enlisted guards and two lieutenants were charged with mistreating prisoners at the Litchfield prison. Johnson and a more experienced lead counsel, Clinton McGee, were able to demonstrate that the abominable conditions at the prison were due to the superior officers. The principal enlisted men charged were given minimal sentences. Johnson seemed to thrive on defending the rights of individuals threatened by higher authorities. While practicing law in Jasper, Alabama, he learned how lawyers could appeal to communities' instincts and sense of fair play—and that lawyers could also use that appeal to people's prejudice and instincts of fear. He spent so much of his life defending the underdog.

Judge Frank Johnson believed that fair play and due process could be achieved with an all-white jury in Alabama. Once, the owner of a black funeral home in Sumter County, Alabama, sent him a photo of a badly beaten and mutilated black man. The funeral home owner sent an accompanying letter, which said that white men had whipped this man to death. Judge Johnson ordered the FBI to investigate this complaint. The evidence showed that the Dials family, who had a plantation, had been cooperating with the local officials to entrap African Americans in a debt system, which enabled the Dials family to have a captive labor force. The black man in the photo had tried to escape but was captured with the help of dogs. The Dials had beaten him with a bullwhip and killed him. Even though the Dials family had a skillful defense lawyer, Judge Johnson was able to bring out testimony that showed that this was a common occurrence on the Dial's farm. The jury returned a guilty verdict.

In large part because of this case and because of the political winds in Alabama, US Attorney General (1953–57). Herbert Brownell was extremely impressed with Judge Frank Johnson and helped expedite his appointment as a federal district judge in the Middle District of Alabama. In addition to the fact that both Brownell and Johnson had worked for President Eisenhower's election and both had friends who had been in the Pi Kappa Alpha fraternity at the University of Alabama, the deciding factor was Johnson's appeal to fundamental fairness as demonstrated in the peonage case.

Shortly after the Senate confirmed Eisenhower's appointment of Judge Johnson, the Autherine Lucy situation at the University of Alabama came to the forefront. Autherine Lucy, an African American woman, was allowed to enroll and enter the University of Alabama after Governor Wallace tried to prevent her from entering and was ordered to make that happen. But then mob disruption occurred and many white southerners thought this would deter any further integration. U.S. District Judge Hobart Grooms overruled the university's racially exclusionary policy and ordered that Autherine Lucy stay at the University of Alabama. A few days later, the university suspended Autherine Lucy from the University of Alabama for her own safety and the safety of other students. Her lawyers filed suit and tried to get her readmitted. Then the University of Alabama expelled Ms. Lucy, and Judge Hobart Grooms upheld their action. Judge Grooms did not receive any help from President Eisenhower, who said he hoped no federal action would be needed. This showed Judge Frank Johnson that the judges themselves were not insulated or protected from mob threats and that there was little hope that they would receive help from the executive branch of the US government. But Judge Johnson was convinced that creative employment of the legal processes could protect individual rights even in the face of public mob protestation.

Not only did Judge Johnson have to overcome the mob distractions and the US executive branch's reticence for action, but also he had to deal with the Southern Manifesto. The Southern congressional leaders declared *Brown* unconstitutional and tried to maintain *Plessy* as the law of the land. Thus, the Southern resistance revolved around their perception that *Brown* dealt only with public school education and had no bearing on anything else, including transportation and the Montgomery bus system. The mayor of Montgomery testified that if segregation were ended, there would be violence and bloodshed beyond belief. Therefore, Judge Johnson felt that Alabama could not wait for further clarification on this issue from the US Supreme Court, and he took it upon himself to extend *Brown* and overturn the Montgomery segregation ordinance. Judge Johnson said, "We cannot in good conscience perform our duty as judges by blindly following the precedent of *Plessy v. Ferguson* when we think that *Plessy v. Ferguson* has been impliedly, though not explicitly, overruled." Judge Johnson felt that lower courts were bound by duty to extend the law into related areas whenever justice was denied. If *Plessy,* which was passed by the US Supreme Court, denied basic American and constitutional rights to Americans, then it was the duty of the courts to rectify the situation. Johnson acted not because he thought that segregation of the races was evil, but because he felt that segregation was against the principles of the constitution as he interpreted them.

It is of interest that although political leaders complained about the decisions of the courts with regard to segregation issues, the actions of these very same leaders were what moved the responsibility for these issues to the judicial system and gave so much power to the courts. It was the massive Southern resistance and the expansive judicial authority that propelled a demand for even more judicial action to end segregation.

Another example of creative judicial response was Judge Johnson's handling of the school segregation issue, which came to his attention in the form of the Macon County School Board segregation case. The Macon County School Board used the Alabama pupil assignment law unconstitutionally to maintain segregation of the races. Judge Johnson initially gave the Macon County School Board time to develop an integration plan. But the Macon County School Board was defiant, and with the help of Governor George Wallace, state troopers used state cars to transport white students to all-white schools, and the governor closed the Tuskegee High School. Judge Frank Johnson ordered the FBI to enter the case and asked them to examine the unconstitutional actions of the Macon County School Board. Then the judge employed this evidence to order an injunctive relief that affected all of the state's school boards. Judge Johnson in effect ordered desegregation in the entire state of Alabama. This order enjoined Governor Wallace and all state school boards not to interfere with the integration of any Alabama public schools. Thus, his order was reparative in nature and went far beyond the original dispute with continuing judicial intervention. Judge Johnson wrote, "If we, as judges, have learned anything from *Brown v. Bd of Education* and its progeny, it is that prohibitory relief alone affords but a hollow protection to the basic and fundamental rights of citizens to equal protection of the law" (quoted in Freyer and Dixon 239). In addition, Judge Johnson said, "Once a constitutional deprivation has been shown, it becomes the duty of the court to render a decree which will as far as possible eliminate the effects of the past deprivations as well as bar like deprivations in the future" (Sikora 174).

The Supreme Court of the United States upheld Johnson's desegregation order for the schools in Montgomery County, and Justice Hugo Black said that the judge's "patience and wisdom" were "written for all to see and read on the pages of the five-year record" (Yackle 21–22; *US v. Montgomery Bd. of Educ.*, 395 US 225, 236 [1969]).

Because of Judge Johnson's uses of injunctive relief, cases were brought before him so that he could employ extended application of these legal techniques. Lawyers brought cases before Johnson's court that sought to have the state of Alabama improve its mental facilities and prison system. Institutions in both of these systems were maintained in deplorable conditions. Judge Johnson appointed a human rights committee made up of Alabama citizens that reported to the court. For example, in *Newman v. Alabama,* there was evidence that state officials were not providing adequate medical care to prisoners. The prisoners were kept in inhumane, overcrowded conditions. Using the human rights committee, Judge Johnson issued orders that forced the state of Alabama to rectify these situations. These changes in judicial tactics were necessary because the state of Alabama defaulted on its responsibility, but community support was required for the changes to be fully effective, and this support did not exist in Alabama. Judge Johnson did not have a road map as to where he was headed, but history continued to drive him in the right direction.

Johnson's cases dealing with the voting rights of all citizens should be considered as well. During his confrontations with Governor Wallace, Judge Johnson developed a "freeze doctrine." He developed the principle that required voter registration boards to use the least qualified white voter to determine the qualification of a black applicant. This thinking formed the basis for the Voting Rights Act of 1965. Judge Johnson was a member of a three-judge court that ruled that the votes of all citizens were to be given equal weight. They held that the Fourteenth Amendment's equal protection clause required the states to adhere to the one person, one vote rule, and this influenced the reapportionment of state legislatures across the nation.

Judge Frank Johnson felt that lawyers had a special function in our society, that of educating the public about the laws: "They must clarify and illumine the distinction between the constitutionally protected rights of expression and violation of the law." He felt that it was the lawyer's duty to "proclaim that the heart of our American system rests in obedience to the laws which protect the individual rights of our citizenry. No system can endure if each citizen is free to choose which laws he will obey. Obedience to the laws we like and defiance of those we dislike is the route to chaos" (Johnson 41, 42).

Freyer and Dixon write, "Thus as the rights revolution proceeded, democracy was at war with itself. Johnson's analogical use of precedent, applications of the proportionality principle, and reparative injunctions generally represented the employment of the wide discretion judicial independence sanctioned to reconcile the tensions within the growing majoritarian consensus" (254).

A judge may be chosen because of the political party issue, but the judicial conduct of that judge is the result of institutional and personal values within the federal judicial system.

8
Rule of Law

Karl Mannheim writes, "Recent studies in the sociology of law once more confirm that the fundamental principle of formal law by which every case must be judged according to the general rational precepts, which have as few exceptions as possible and are based on logical subsumptions, obtains only for the liberal competitive phase of capitalism" (180).

The "rule of law" means that a government is bound by rules fixed beforehand—rules that make it possible for the people in power to know with certainty how they can use their authority. Albert Venn Dicey, in his *Introduction to the Study of Law of the Constitution,* states that the rule of law "means, in the first place, the absolute supremacy or predominance of regular law as opposed to the influence of arbitrary power, and excludes the existence of arbitrariness, of prerogative, or even of wide discretionary authority on the part of government" (8th edition, 1915, 198). Adherence to the rule of law can never be perfectly achieved mainly because legislators are fallible. History has shown that discretion left to the executive branch of government has to be reduced (Hayek 112–16). Citizens have to know their ambitions will not be frustrated by the whims of government executives. The rule of law has to be protected from arbitrary government.

The state should establish the rules that apply to general situations. But the individuals in a society must have freedom to make decisions that affect their activities and should be able to use their knowledge to make their own plans. The more that the state plans, the more difficult life will be for individuals. When the government knows which groups of people will be affected by its policies and what the effects of its actions will be, then the government cannot be impartial. When a government takes sides on an issue and tries to impose its values on a group of people, it chooses the end for its citizens. The government should try to assist its citizens, not impose its will on the citizens. And so it was with the Nazi government, which decided that its Jewish citizens were subhuman and should be eliminated and utilized the rule of law to accomplish its goals. Thus, the power of the state was utilized to influence and persuade all branches of the government, including the executive, the legislative, and even the judicial, that the values selected by the government were to be imposed and utilized. Judges were then coerced into confirming the judicial validity of the government's actions. And yet, legal means were employed by Adolf Hitler and the Nazi government to enable them to gain control of the government. It is important to realize that the decline of the rule of law had been going on for some time prior to Hitler's rise in power, given that the previous government had been engaged in totalitarian planning, and Hitler just had to extend those concepts and complete the work. It is that rule of law that protects the citizens from an arbitrary government but citizens have to be vigilant so that none of the leaders can abuse their power and position. But the power of the state can be influential even on the decisions made by judges.

In recent years, various courts have attempted to avoid any reliance on historical records. Sometimes when the courts have referred to history, they have relied on mis-portrayals, which have been manipulated to give the appearance of the approval of the founders of this country. And so at times the courts and these misrepresentations of history have influenced judges. Frequently, whenever there is a court case involving the First Amendment, there is reference to the Fourteenth Amendment. By referring to the Fourteenth Amendment in this way, the courts adopt a mechanism that permits the federal government to intervene in all practices of the states.

There were three amendments to the US Constitution after the Civil War. The Thirteenth Amendment was passed in 1865, and this abolished slavery. Some of the Southern dissidents objected and then took the position that former slaves would be legally free, but the former slaves should not be granted the rights of citizens of a state. Congress then passed the Fourteenth Amendment, which in fact gave all freed slaves the privileges and rights of citizens of states and of the nation. Then the Fifteenth Amendment was passed in 1870, which gave these freed slaves the right to vote and participate in all political affairs. Even though most of the courts recognized these amendments, they did not uniformly uphold them. The courts were following the judicial principle described by John Marshall in *McCullough v. Maryland:* "An exposition of the Constitution deliberately established by legislative acts ... ought not to be lightly disregarded" (*McCullough v. Maryland,* 4 Wheaton 316, 401 [1819]). This gave credence to judges' approach of determining the legislative intent for a law when and before they applied it.

In the Fourteenth Amendment, the intent of the Congress was to make recently freed slaves citizens of the state in which they lived (Barton 203–7). Could the courts and judges manage to completely separate the wording from its intent? In several cases, the courts did just that, including *Cantwell v. Connecticut* (310 US 296 [1940])., *Murdock v. Pennsylvania* (319 US 105 [1943])., and *Everson v. Board of Education* (330 US 1 [1947]). Many judges said that the purpose of the Fourteenth Amendment was to limit the states not only on racial civil rights cases, but also on numerous other issues in the Bill of Rights. They then said that the First Amendment was to limit every state and not just the federal government as was originally intended. Even though many courts used the Fourteenth Amendment as legal justification for involvement in the issues of states, history really shows that the Fourteenth Amendment did not give any basis for this interference. So it is easy to see how most of the judges in the state of Alabama ruled one way and a few others ruled another and relied on what they felt was the right decision to make.

Further elucidation of why judges saw the law differently requires a review of judicial history in Alabama. Article III in the US Constitution established the separation of the judiciary but gave to the Congress the right to determine the size of the Supreme Court and the creation of the lower courts. The Judiciary Act of 1789 provided for the creation of district courts for each state and assigned circuit-riding duties to the Supreme Court (Freyer and Dixon 257–63). One of the purposes of this act was to provide a mechanism for monitoring federal judges and the laws of the various states. The Alabama courts attempted to balance the national values with the state values, but most all-constitutional opinions favored states' rights and local economic issues.

After the Civil War, the authority of the Southern states became subordinate to federal power in a gradual manner. During the Reconstruction period, the US Congress enlarged the jurisdiction of the federal judiciary with the Removal Act of 1875. This legislation encouraged litigants to remove their cases from the state courts to the federal courts. Initially, Alabama judges used this new authority to protect individuals under federal laws and the Fourteenth and Fifteenth Amendments. But Congressional Republicans and many in the North allowed the Reconstruction to collapse, and eventually the South won the peace. Alabama's federal courts continued in their attempts to defend African Americans from peonage, which led to opinions from the Supreme Court invalidating efforts to reinstitute slavery by another name. But efforts to prevent the establishment of Jim Crow laws in the South were unsuccessful. Alabama's federal judges sustained the Interstate Commerce Commission's regulation of the railroads. The Alabama federal judges did not support the Tennessee Valley Authority. President Franklin Roosevelt appointed a new judge for the Northern District of Alabama, and afterward, the Alabama federal courts supported the Social Security Act of 1935. Following *Brown v. Board of Education* (1954)., Alabama's federal courts ended the Montgomery bus boycott; upheld constitutionality of the various civil rights and voting rights laws; established the one man, one vote concept with respect to legislative apportionment; engineered a peaceful resolution of the Selma-to- Montgomery march; brought about relief for the rights of mental patients and prisoners; and defined affirmative action (Freyer and Dixon 258–59).

Although the lives of the freedmen and freedwomen were adversely affected when the Reconstruction period faded in failure, the new economic and social issues came more under the jurisdiction of the federal courts. With the expansion of sociological laws came the increased willingness of the federal courts to improve the lives of African Americans who were subject to the whims of the Jim Crow laws. Social laws and psychology did influence the decisions of judges. It became accepted that personal elements and experience affected judges' judgment, and this was not separate from institutional factors.

According to Freyer and Dixon, "Usually internal institutional factors interacting with personal, nonparty values were the most important influences shaping a judge's decisions. The necessary distinction that needed to be made was between personal values derived from family and social background on the one hand and formal partisan party principles on the other. Accordingly, the judge's use of discretion to determine a particular decision reflected personal values and federal judiciary's indigenous institutional culture" (263).

Despite the resistance of public officials in Alabama to the growth of federal influence and decisions, federal judiciary influence grew, and these federal judges have been able to strengthen the individual rights of the citizens of Alabama and democracy.

9
Becoming Alabama

Becoming Alabama is a partnership involving the Alabama Department of Archives and History; the First White House of the Confederacy in Montgomery, Alabama; and other Alabama organizations to commemorate the anniversaries of several important events, such as the bicentennial of the Creek War and the War of 1812, the sesquicentennial of the Civil War, and the fiftieth anniversary of major events in the struggle for civil rights. Because this book is concerned with events of the last two periods, it is appropriate to discuss this project in more detail, given that Alabama was at the epicenter of so much of this aspect of American history. There will be many sesquicentennial events planned in Alabama in 2011. Re-enactors will appear at Fort Morgan, which played a significant role in protecting Mobile during the Civil War. There will be increased tourism at the Confederate Memorial Park, and new plays about these subjects will be performed at the Alabama Shakespeare Festival. The Birmingham Museum of Art will display Civil War–related works of art. In addition, the First White House of the Confederacy is planning several events throughout 2011. Although not officially a part of the Becoming Alabama events, there also is now a new musical starting on Broadway about the Scottsboro boys scandal.

Most certainly there will be an event at Alabama's Confederate Monument, which was constructed in 1886. Judge Thomas Goode Jones gave a very famous speech there on April 27, 1874, that was heard all over the American nation. This speech has been compared to one given by General Douglas McArthur at West Point and to that given by Rev. Martin Luther King Jr. at the Lincoln Memorial in 1963. Some of Jones's speech is reproduced here:

It has often been the fate of people in other climes to mourn defeat and slain warriors, while bending under the yoke of the captive on the shores of a foreign land. No picture of human woe is more touching than that of the nation "that wept by the rivers of Babylon" o'er its children slaughtered—its cities sacked and overthrown.

But the cup was not for us. We, thank God, stand in unshackled manhood beside these graves, and under native skies, to render fitting tribute to the dead—tribute worthy of the men—tribute worthy of the Cause for which they died.

And that Cause—shall I wrong it by arguing its Right, or seek to trace in the misty tomes of by-gone days the purity of its source? Nay! The law, which nerved these men to die, was graven on their inmost souls by the finger of the Almighty. He instilled in them love of native land. He gave them heroic aspirations and lofty thoughts. He was the author of their manhood and their courage. He was the Ruler of the Storm and King of Battles, and in His wisdom, the storm was permitted to lash about them, who shall dare condemn these men obeying God-given instincts, they, breasting the storm, marched down the pathway of duty to death?

What need has that Cause of the tongue of man or pen of poet? The graves of the dead, "severed far and wide, by mount, and stream, and sea," and hallowed half a continent, are its mightiest defenders.

In the old World, marble and bronze perpetuate the deeds of the emperor—the chieftain dead in victory. With pomp and ceremony they bury the great in the shadow and mildew of the Abbey. We reverently lay down all our dead out in the sunshine, under the shade of the trees. But where in all the eastern lands—where , at Rome or Greece—where at Warsaw or Marathon, may the patriot weep beside the untitled graves of the martyrs, gone down in freedom's cause? In the New World, no such mournful enquiry rises to the lips. These impressive ceremonies—the solemn hush falling on all hearts—the thronging of the living in the "silent cities of the dead," that sanctify, with their glory, all the land stretching from the heights of Arlington to the utmost shores of Rio Grande, tell, alas, their own mournful story.

Brass and marble crumble. Time, with corroding hand, changes chronicles of glory into heaps of ashes. But these tombs will not pass away. They are monuments built of the soul—glorious protests of Valor and Truth against fate. They are builded not "of the earth, earthy," but of the soul— sublime, immortal. Simple and humble though they be, the hand of love can add nothing to their grandeur—nor the tongue of eloquence aught to their teachings.

At Thermopylae, a monument towers to Heaven, on which is inscribed, "Stranger, go tell at Lacedemon, that we lie here in obedience to her laws!" And when the dead are brought back from glorious war, there was appointed unto them, by Grecian law, special days of mourning and high honors. Do we, living in a land of more than one Thermopylae, need any cold words chiseled on stone, to tell us for what these men died? All human law sinks into nothingness beside the great command that brings us here. Not alone did it bid us come when first they "laid the dear dumb warriors down"—but forever in the flowers of each returning spring, it beckons all hearts to these tombs.

The simple recital of the deeds of these men—their lives—their deaths—even now thrills all Christendom. There were no depths of misfortune they did not sound—no path of duty they left untrod. They defied time, the elements, man— all things, save their honor and their God. Fate could not quench their valor, nor death quell their convictions.

The Great Eternal Pen has registered up in Heaven their weary midnight marches—the gnawing of hunger and the weakness that comes of famine—the agony of that hope deferred that maketh the heart sick—the supplicating prayer for a cup of cold water, and the parching fever—the blood stained tracks like those at Valley Forge—the wasting of the trenches—the silent vigils of the outpost—the last sigh in the hospital—the unseen death on the picket-post—the sublime end in the forlorn hope—the glorious sunset of manhood in the arms of victory.

Girt on the east and south by a hostile sea, that floated no friendly ensign—traversed everywhere by broad rivers— corralled in by a brave and warlike people for more than a thousand miles on its northern and western confines—well might the world pause in mute admiration on that April day, thirteen years ago, when the Sunny South, upstarting, faced a world in arms! For long years these men watched the seashore and girdling native land with wall of fire and steel, twice forced their banners to the Ohio. Twice across the Potomac their valor almost reared, on the shores of the little stream that runs hard-by Sharpsburg, and on the heights of Gettysburg, a new nation amongst the people of the earth.

They lit all the sea-shore with their glory, and sanctified all the mountains and plains with their dead bodies. More than one Austerlitz illumined their pathway—no Ulm, no Sedau darkened their end. That end came not until the armies were so worn by battle and toil, that the colors almost twined above the thin line. They fell, not like the old tree, limb by limb till it toppled down, but like the giant oak against which the earthquake hurls the mountain side—not until every root and fibre was shattered and torn.

Such my countrymen, is a feeble outline of the men whose memory we this day embalm in fond affection!

The dead have "passed from the sphere of earth's wrongs and the earth's reparations." No more will the sheen of the warrior's spear brighten the green woods—ne'er again will his glad steps pass over the threshold to the hearthstone. The bivouac fire has flickered and gone out—the tents are all folded, and the warrior waits the great final reveille.

There remains to us but their fame—the widow and the orphan. Who that has ever touched elbows in the line of battle, but has heard the whispered prayer:

"Whatever fate those forms may show,

Loved with a passion almost wild,

By day-by night-in joy or woe-

By fears oppressed, or hopes beguilded,

From every danger—every foe-

Oh God! Protect my wife and child."

Have we healed all the wounds that would yield to our touch? Have we fed all the lips that lacked bread, and cheered all the souls that lacked light? Have we watched and waited and prayed for discernment to give, with genuine love, that which the dead can not ask for the little ones?

'Tis said that the dead some times hover around the hearthstone that mourns them. But, be that as it may be, one by one, messengers leave us for the unknown land. Not long since a noble spirit, on this very spot, uttered words of heroic manhood in eulogy of his dead comrades, but like them, too, he has "crossed over the river and rested under the shade of the trees."

Think you that he bore those dwellers beyond the stars no joy in the tidings of what his eye had seen and his heart felt here? What greater reward need we than the thought!

The same sun that mellows the landscape here, lingers lovingly o'er a new made grave on the banks of the Chattahoochee. The gently white hands that first toiled to shelter the Confederate orphans are folded to rest. The pure spirit which first whispered with seraphic love of this Memorial Day, gazes into a face which makes glorious her own, midst throngs of angels.

Her whole life was but "to heal the sick, to lift the lowly, to bind the broken." Who shall tell her reward? To what shall I liken her? "The violet—the dew drop—the evening star—the gentle rain—Through all symbols I search for her sweetness in vain."

And while we ponder thus, the mind carries us Northward, where the tombs—not of our dead—are whiter than the sands of the sea, and more numerous than the stars in the Heavens. In them lie men of the same race as ourselves—who spoke the same language, and worshipped the same God. Fond mothers sent them to battle, and tender tears and agonizing prayers watched their pathway. They followed a flag that was as dear to them as was to us the "star-crossed banner that has long since taken its flight to greet the warrior's soul"; and he that worthily speaks for the dead or the living, must say that no feeling of hate to the northern dead or *those who mourn them, pervades this Memorial Day! "One touch of pity makes the whole world kin." From scenes like this, where the warring sections mourn their dead, let the statesman draw inspiration to guide the living.*

And while honoring ourselves and our dead, let us do all that men may do to hasten the coming of that great day when peace and goodwill shall once more prevail over all the land.

But there are duties that will not wait the coming of that day. Before the bar of history we must appear as "rebels" or as "patriots." Ours be it to see that no rude hand writes the record of our dead, or scrawls the word "traitor" on their tombstones.

No, not ours! But to you, oh women of the South—you who were ever "last at the cross and first at the grave"—you who sustained and honored and cheered these men to the last—to you, more noble than the Spartan woman who gave her tresses for bow-strings and her girdle for swordbelt—to you, who dared all the danger and sorrow of the strife and shared none of the wild joys—to you, who ne'er murmured, save when your warrior lost faith—to you, God has left the memory of the dead!

A glorious and noble past is a nation's highest treasure. All that makes man great is fed in the contemplation of unselfish heroism. "Honor thy father and thy mother, that thy days may be long in the land which the Lord thy God giveth thee," was written not alone of those whose name and blood we inherit, but also of the noble and great of the forefathers—the founders of the State. The nation may neglect the command and forfeit the promise, as well as the child. 'Tis something akin to the immortals that makes us long not to be altogether unworthy of the fame of our ancestors. Lycurgus has said that the character of the child, worthily reared, is formed by the age of seven; however this may be, it is certain that if the child respect himself he must honor his father. 'Tis your God-given mission to fashion the man in the boy, and nurture the true woman in the girl. 'Tis yours to feed the manly instinct—to train the young eagle to the flight of the old. Then gather around this spot, when the flowers sweeten the air and the song of birds makes melody, with the children that cluster around your knee, and tell them the story of their fathers and brothers. Teach them that "the man is noblest when he dies for man"—that their fathers were heroes and patriots, worthy of and winning the admiration of the gods. And if any wound their young hearts with epithet against the dead, point to the answer.

When the victor of Chancellorville resigned his soul to the angels who bore him in their upward flight o'er that "tangled wilderness" in whose solitude the dead lay yet unburied, and the shrieks of the wounded and the thunder of the cannon were yet unhushed, and was joined by the souls reft from the bodies that lay wrapped in the blue and in the grey—when the throng with reverential awe approached the Great White Throne, and the God of Battles crowned him, midst the angels and archangels, think you that in all the corridors of Heaven any dared whisper "treason?" Or when the blue-eyed "boy captain," who wrapped his colors round his breast at Franklin, and on a stormy night—made calm by Christian resignation—entered into his rest, think you that the pen of the recording angel had traced any line of disapproval in the Golden Chronicle that told of the cause to which he gave his life and his faith?

What may not be muttered in Heaven of our dead must soon pass away from earth. Until that hour strikes, be it yours to keep undefiled the memory of the dead! And this struggle—was it all in vain? Is there nothing come back to us out of all this woe?

What has become of all the deeds, all the heroism of the unknown and unmarked dead—those who had no rank to attract the eyes of the country—no interest savoring of earth but what bid them flee the conflict—no guiding star but duty—no plaudits but the echoes of their own faithful hearts?

Is there nothing to bless us in return for all the wealth of youth we gave—for all the agonies we dared?

Nothing can perish. The wasting substance in matter will soon greet us in a thousand blossoms, and mingle in a thousand living forms. How, then, shall actions, crystallized out of the souls and prayers and tears of millions, pass utterly away? Methinks they still linger about these "God's acres"—that they float everywhere around us—in the air— in the clouds—in the river—in the rain—on the mountain top—and, like the lightning now slumbering in the skies, will yet illuminate with a blaze of glory all the Heavens!

We failed—"That's best
Which God sends
'Twas His will—it is ours"

But who is there that looks on this scene, but feels "that love, though love be given in vain, is yet lovely?"

"No stream from its source
Flows seaward, how lone so ever its course,
But What some land is gladdened.
No star ever rose and set without
Some influence somewhere.
No life can be pure in its purpose
And strong in its strife,
And all life not be purer and stronger thereby."
"The gathering hand of time puts in the sickle," and soon all the comrades of the dead, like them, will rest in the

silent furrows of the fight. Let us so act, that when one by one
the living soldier shall join the ranks of the dead, he shall
carry with him remembrance of no act which would make us
accounted unworthy of "the grand army of martyrs which is
still marching onward beyond the stars."

> "But the sun sinks in the west, and
> We must yet strew our flowers—
> And you,
> Whom this song can not reach
> With its transient breath,
> Deaf ears that are stopped with
> The brown dust of death,
> Blind eyes that are dark to your
> Own deathless glory,
> Silent hearts that are heedless of
> The praised murmured o'er ye,
> Sleep deep! Sleep in peace! Sleep
> In memory ever!
> Wrapt each soul in the deeds of
> Its deathless endeavor,
> Till the great Final Peace shall be
> Struck through the world:
> Till the stars be recalled and the
> Firmament furled!
> What is worth living for, is worth
> Dying for too
> And therefore, all honor brave
> Hearts; unto you
> Who have fallen that Freedom,
> More fair by your death,
> A pilgrim may walk where your
> Blood on her path
> Leads her steps to your graves!" (Eidsmoe 82–94).

As this journey through Alabama comes to an end, let's review
the one sentence that sums it all up, spoken by Atticus in *To Kill a*

Mockingbird: "The one place where a man ought to get a square deal is in the courtroom, be he any color of the rainbow" (H. Lee295). Also, Dorothy Rabinowitz, in her book *No Crueler Tyrannies: Accusation, False Witness, and Other Terrors of Our Times,* cites Louis de Secondat: "There is no crueler tyranny than that which is perpetrated under the shield of law and the name of justice" (Rabinowitz vi). "Through the years, some judges have convinced many people—including themselves—that they use esoteric materials and techniques to build an edifice of doctrines unmarked by wilfulness, politics, or ignorance" (Posner 3).

In this book we visited the courtroom of Chief Justice George Stone and learned of his ruling that lawyers are accountable for their actions and mistakes. He said, "It surely cannot be successfully maintained, that lawyers are a privileged case, not responsible for even the grossest want of skill" (Brantley 108). Judge Stone also ruled that the Confederate conscription laws gave the Confederacy the right to draft soldiers directly from Alabama. Without this authority, the Confederacy surely would have exhausted its supply of soldiers and would not have been able to prosecute the war. This courageous decision did cost Judge Stone his position on the court.

In the courtroom of Judge Thomas Goode Jones, we saw that his most significant contribution was the first code of ethics. Judge Jones opposed laws that subjected black farmers to peonage or imprisonment for debt. He also opposed the Alabama convict lease system, which added revenues to the state of Alabama. He fought against lynching and felt that the state of Alabama owed its prisoners a trial and sufficient protection while they were in state custody. He supported legislation that increased the funding of education for all citizens, black and white. He tried to increase the ability of black citizens to serve in the militia.

While in the courtroom of Judge James E. Horton, we reviewed the history of the trials and retrials of the Scottsboro boys. Judge Horton from the beginning said these boys were innocent, and he set aside one guilty verdict and showed great courage by ordering yet another trial. As a result, Judge Horton lost his judgeship in the following election.

Perhaps the most active courtroom we visited was the one in which Judge Frank M. Johnson presided. Judge Johnson ruled that the segregation employed by the Montgomery bus system was unconstitutional. He approved of the march from Selma to Montgomery whereby the black citizens petitioned Governor George Wallace for their civil rights. He desegregated public schools and colleges in Alabama, as well as parks, libraries, train and bus depots, airports, restaurants, restrooms, and the Alabama state police. He sent the killers of civil rights worker Viola Liuzzo to jail. He tried to protect the Freedom Riders and ordered that the state of Alabama improve the prison system and the mental hospitals.

Finally, we learned about Becoming Alabama, the commemoration of some of the sentinel events in the history of both the United States of America and the state of Alabama. This commemoration is not a celebration of the Civil War and slavery, but rather represents a time for all of us to remember and think about our heritage and history, so that we can better deal with all unfinished business and problems that stem from that period. Becoming Alabama is commemorating the beginning of the Civil War, the end of slavery, the end of the convict lease system, the end of Jim Crow laws, and the struggle for civil rights. So with that in mind, it is hoped that this book and the events staged by the First White House of the Confederacy will accomplish these goals of commemorating Alabama history. The state of Alabama has given the world the gift of civil progression toward full democracy for all citizens.

Bibliography

Bailey, Richard. *Neither Carpetbaggers nor Scalawags: Black Officeholders during the Reconstruction of Alabama, 1867–1878,* 2nd ed. Montgomery,Alabama, Richard Bailey Publishers 1993.

Barton, David. *Original Intent: The Courts, the Constitution, and Religion,* 5th ed. Aledo, TX: Wallbuilder Press, 1996.

Baum, Lawrence. *Judges and Their Audiences: A Perspective on Judicial Behavior Princeton,New Jersey,Princeton Press.* 2006, Chapter one.

Blackmon, Douglas A. *Slavery by Another Name: The Re-Enslavement of Black Americans from the Civil War to World War II.* New York: Anchor Books, 2009.

Brandt, Allen M. *Racism and Research: The Case of the Tuskegee Syphilis Experiment.* Hastings Center Report 8 (1978).: 26.

Brantley, William. *Chief Justice Stone.* Birmingham, AL: Birmingham Publishing, 1943.

Browne, Ray B., and Lawrence A. Kreiser Jr. *The Civil War and Reconstruction.* Westport, CT: Greenwood Press, 2003.

Caffey, George. "George Washington Stone, 1811–1894." In *Great American Lawyers,* edited by William Draper Lewis, vol. 6, 165–93. Philadelphia: John C. Winston: 1907–09.

Cardozo, Benjamin N. *The Nature of the Judicial Process, The Storrs Lectures at Yale University, Yale University Press, New Haven, CT, p* 13, April 19, 1921.

Carter, Dan T. *Scottsboro—A Tragedy of the American South.* Baton Rouge: Louisiana State University Press, 1979

Dicey,Albert Venn. *Introduction to the Study of Law of the Constitution,* 8th ed. London: Macmillan, 1915,p198.

DuBose, John Witherspoon,*A Historian's Tribute to Thomas Goode Jones;* reprinted from XIV:1 Alabama Law. (January 1953).

Eidsmore, John A. *Warrior, Statesman, Jurist for the South: The Life, Legacy, and Law of Thomas Goode Jones, Harrisonburg, Virginia, Sprinkle Publications,2003*

Freyer, Tony, and Timothy Dixon. *Democracy and Judicial Independence: A History of the Federal Courts of Alabama, 1820–1994.* Brooklyn, NY: Carlson Publishing, 1995.

Friedman, Barry. "The Politics of Judicial Review." *Texas Law Review* 257 (2005).

Hayek, Friedrich A. von *The Road to Serfdom.* Chicago: University of Chicago Press, 2007,p112,113,114

Henshaw, Virgil, *Albert Einstein: Philosopher-Scientist,* 1949, edited by Paul A. Schipp.

Horton, Mary Edge. "Alabama's Code of Ethics." Alabama Law 197 (March 2000).: 130.

Hutcheson, Joseph C. "The Judgment Intuitive: The Function of the 'Hunch' in Judicial Decisions." *Cornell Law Quarterly* 14 (1929).: 274, 275–76.

Jenkins, Sally, and John Stauffer. *The State of Jones., New York,* Doubleday, 200

Johnson, Frank M. "The Attorney and the Supremacy of Law." *Georgia Law Review* (1966).: 41–42.

Jones, Thomas Goode. Address at Oakwood Cemetery, Montgomery, Alabama, April 27, 1874. *Alabama Bible Society Quarterly* 11, no. 2 (April 1955).: 2–6. Also in Eidsmore 82–94.

Jones, Thomas Goode. "Salutation." *Daily Picayune*, June 11, 1868, 2.

Jones, W. B. *Anecdotes about Governor Thomas G. Jones of Alabama, supra* n. 65, at 16–17).

Jones, W.B. *Burgwin-Jones* supra n.1 at 106-107

Kennedy, Robert F., Jr. *Judge Frank M. Johnson, Jr.* New York: G. P. Putnam's Sons, 1978.

Kidder, Rushworth M. *Moral Courage.,New York,* Harper 2005.

King, ML, *Remaining Awake Through a Great Revolution*, 1968

Kritzer, Herbert M. "Law Is the Mere Continuation of Politics by Different Means: American Judicial Selection in the Twenty-First Century." *DePaul Law Review* 56 (2007).: 423, 461–64.

Kushner, Harold S. *Conquering Fear—Living Boldly in an Uncertain World.* New York: Knopf, 2009.

Lee, Gus, with Diane Elliott-Lee. *Courage: The Backbone of Leadership.* San Francisco: Jossey-Bass, 2006.

Lee, Harper. *To Kill a Mockingbird.* New York: Grand Central Publishing, 1960.

Linder, Douglas O. "'The Scottsboro Boys' Trials: 1931–1937." *Famous Trials.* http://www.law.umkc.edu/faculty/projects/ FTrials/scottsboro/scottsb.htm.

MacMillan, Malcolm Cook. "Thomas Goode Jones 1844–1914: Warrior, Statesman, and Jurist." Address at Alabama Polytechnic Institute, Auburn, Alabama, p50-51

Mannheim, Karl. *Man and Society in an Age of Reconstruction, Collected Works of Karl Mannheim, Volume 2, Routledge, New York, 2001,* op. cit, p. 180.

Manning, Sherman D., *American Dream, A Search For Justice*, 2003, p125

McGarvie, Blythe J. *Shaking the Globe: Courageous Decision-Making in a Changing World.* Hoboken, NJ: Wiley, 2009.

McGee, Celia. "The Open Road Wasn't Quite Open to All." *New York Times*, August 23, 2010, the Arts, C1, C2.

McKensie, Robert H. "Farrah's Future: The First One Hundred Years of the University of Alabama Law School, 1872–1972." *Alabama Law Review* 25 (Fall 1972).: 121.

McMurry, Richard M. *Virginia Military Institute Alumni in the Civil War: In Bello Praesidium.* Lynchburg, VA: H. E. Howard, 1999.

Posner, Richard A. *How Judges Think.* Cambridge, MA: Harvard University Press, 2008.

Rabinowitz, Dorothy. *No Crueler Tyrannies: Accusation, False Witness, and Other Terrors of our Times.* New York: Free Press, 2003.

Randall, Horace, and Christine Garrett, eds. *The Alabama Guide: Our People, Resources, and Government.* Montgomery, AL: Publications Office of the Department of Archives and History, 2009.

Reynolds, David S., *John Brown, Abolitionist,* New York, Alfred A. Knopf, 2005

Rumore, Pat Boyd. *The Story of Lawyers in Alabama.* Dallas, TX: Taylor Publishing, 2010.

Rogers, William Warren, Robert David Ward, Leah Rawls Atkins, and Wayne Flint. *Alabama: The History of a Deep South State.* Tuscaloosa: University of Alabama Press, 1994.

Schauer, Frederick. "Formalism." *Yale Law Journal* 97 (1988).: 509.

Scottsboro Boys. http://en.wikipedia.org/wiki/Scottsboro_Boys.

Seiller, Cotton. *Republic of Drivers: A Cultural History of Automobility in America.*, University of Chicago Press, Chicago, Illinois, 240pages, 2008

Sikora, Frank. *The Judge: The Life and Opinion of Alabama's Frank M. Johnson, Jr.* Montgomery, AL: New South Books, 2007.

Society of Pioneers of Montgomery and Their Ancestors. *Pioneers, Past & Present 1855–2001.* Montgomery, AL: Society of Pioneers, 2001.

Stewart, John Craig. *The Governors of Alabama.* Gretna, LA: Pelican, 1975.

Tamanaha, Brian Z. "How an Instrumental View of Law Corrodes the Rule of Law." 56*DePaul Law Review469,490* (2007).

Washington, Harriet A. *Medical Apartheid: The Dark History of Medical Experimentation on Black Americans from Colonial Times to the Present.* New York: Anchor Books, 2006.

Wiesel, Elie, Nobel Acceptance Speech, 1968

Wistrich, Andrew J., Chris Guthrie, and Jeffrey J. Rachlinski. "Can Judges Ignore Inadmissible and Formation? The Difficulty of Deliberating Disregarding." *University of Pennsylvania Law Review* 153 (2005).: 1251.

Wood, Mattie Pegues. *The Life of St. John's Parish: A History of St. John's Episcopal Church from 1834 to 1955.* Montgomery, AL: Black Belt Press, 1990

Yackle, Larry W. *Reform and Regret, The Story of Federal Judicial Involvement in the Alabama Prison System,* Oxford University Press, Oxford, England, 1989, p20-21

Legal References

Bain v State 70 Ala 4. Myers v. State 1878 62 Ala 599,1881

Cleveland v. State 86 Ala 1,1888

Dawson Perry v. New Orleans, Mobile and Chattanooga Railroad ,1867

Dawson v.Strawbridge and Mays XXXIX Ala 367,WL 511,1864

Hill v. Confederate States , XXXVIII Ala 4565

McManus v State 36 Ala 285,1860

Strawbridge and Mays v.State XXXIX Ala 367,WL 511,1864

Boyd vs. The State LIII Ala 601 & 615 53 Ala 601,WL 261,1875

Browder v Gayle 142 F. Supp. 707,1956Lee v Macon County Board of Education 231 Federal Supp page 743,1958

Frontiero v Laird 341 F. Supp 201,1972

James v Wallace 386 F. Supp 8151974

NAACP v Allen340 F. Supp 703,1972

US v Frazer—317 F. supp 1079,1970

Wyatt v Stickney 344 F. supp 387,1971